THE
PEOPLE
OF
GREAT RUSSIA

A Psychological Study

by

Geoffrey Gorer

and

John Rickman

The Norton Library

W · W · NORTON & COMPANY · INC ·

NEW YORK

TO THE LIVING MEMORY
OF
RUTH FULTON BENEDICT
1877–1948

FIRST PUBLISHED IN THE NORTON LIBRARY 1962

W. W. Norton & Company, Inc. is also the publisher of
the works of Erik H. Erikson, Otto Fenichel, Karen Horney and
Harry Stack Sullivan, and the principal works of Sigmund Freud.

Printed in the United States of America

ACKNOWLEDGEMENTS

The research embodied in the section 'The Psychology of Great Russians' was undertaken as part of my work for the Columbia University project, Research in Contemporary Cultures, which was inaugurated by the late Professor Ruth Benedict in 1947. I wish to express my gratitude for permission to publish the results of this research.

Research in Contemporary Cultures was conducted in area seminars, and I wish to express my gratitude and sense of intellectual obligation to my collaborators in the Russian group: Dr. S. Benet, Mr. N. Calas, Dr. N. Leites, Miss M. Marcovitz, Dr. M. Mead, Dr. B. Schaffner, Dr. I. Telberg, Dr. M. Wolfenstein, Miss R. Zoglin, and others.

An earlier and shorter version of this section has been published in the American *Eastern European and Slavic Review* under the title 'Some Aspects of the Psychology of the People of Great Russia'. I wish to express my gratitude to the editors of this journal for permission to re-use some of the material.

I wish to thank the following authors and publishers for permission to use quotations from their copyright books: Oriana Atkinson and the Bobbs-Merrill Co., *Over at Uncle Joe's*; N. Berdyaev and Geoffrey Bles, *The Russian Idea*; George S. Counts and Nucia P. Lodge and Victor Gollancz, *I Want to be Like Stalin*; Melanie Klein and the Hogarth Press, *Contributions to Psychoanalysis*, 1921–1945.

GEOFFREY GORER

ACKNOWLEDGEMENTS

Earlier versions of some of the material in 'Russian Camera Obscura' have appeared in the *Lancet* in 1938 (under the pseudonym 'Vratch'), the *Atlantic Monthly*, *The Nation* (New York), and *The Nation* (London) in 1919.

JOHN RICKMAN

CONTENTS

INTRODUCTION AND INTRODUCTION—1961
by Geoffrey Gorer

RUSSIAN CAMERA OBSCURA
Ten Sketches of Russian Peasant Life (1916–1918)
by John Rickman

THE PSYCHOLOGY OF GREAT RUSSIANS
by Geoffrey Gorer

APPENDICES

INTRODUCTION

'The Russian nation is a new and wonderful phenomenon in the history of mankind. The character of the people differs to such a degree from that of the other Europeans that their neighbours find it impossible to diagnose them.'

F. DOSTOIEVSKY

I

THIS BOOK represents a portion of a co-operative attempt to understand the people of Great Russia; to isolate and analyse the principal motives which can be discerned as informing and underlying their typical behaviour, whether this behaviour be that of large groups as described by historians and economists, or of fictional characters which have been described by Great Russian novelists, poets and playwrights and accepted by their compatriots as true or probable. Concurrently it is an attempt to explore the means by which these motives are elicited and maintained in the majority of the new members who are added to the society by birth, so that the society maintains its identity and consistency through time.

This last statement entails certain assumptions which are, in the strictest logic, unprovable but which seem at least to me highly probable. It assumes that the term 'society' implies more than a group of people inhabiting a more or less closely defined portion of the earth's surface and speaking one or more identified languages; it assumes that there are more than geographic and linguistic connexions between the people who inhabited England (or Great Russia, or anywhere else) one or two centuries ago, and those who inhabit the same places to-day.

These connexions (it is assumed) are maintained by the fact that all the members of a society share aspects of a culture, in the anthropological sense of the word: that is to say, shared patterns of learned behaviour by means of which their fundamental biological drives are transformed into social needs and gratified through the appropriate institutions, which also define the permitted and the forbidden.

'Natural' man is a figment of the philosopher's imagination. Never and nowhere has man passed infancy without the constraints and guidance of social rules. This is true even of the technically most primitive groups we know about, living on the margin of subsistence. To take a simple example, no society anywhere satisfies the hunger of its members according attention only to the individual physiological rhythms and the raw material available. All societies choose some foods and reject others (as unclean, disgusting, ritually impure, unfit for men, &c., &c.); the selected foods are (with slight exceptions) never eaten when found, but are brought to appropriate places, prepared in prescribed manner, and eaten at relatively fixed periods of the day, usually in groups who are socially formally related to one another. If by chance an individual were to eat food that his society defines as unclean or disgusting, it is likely to be followed by profound physiological disturbances, even though the neighbours across the frontier eat such food daily with impunity.

The question why any given society accepts or rejects any given food is almost always unanswerable; and it is usually unprofitable to ask such questions of origin. It can be easily observed that the people of Great Britain (or the United States) treat goat's milk as disgusting, whereas the people of Spain and Italy drink it regularly; that mussels are generally eaten on the east coast of the Atlantic and clams on the west, though both types of shell-fish occur on both coasts; that on one side of the English Channel only one type of wild fungus is normally eaten, whereas on the other more than a score are looked for and enjoyed; and so on, almost endlessly. Although historical reasons, religious beliefs or the like rationalizations may be adduced for given examples, there are far more which are passed over as self-evident. As far as I know, no European society has evolved social explanations why dogs are not eaten; in Asia, where some societies do eat dogs, those who do not have (many of them) laws or myths justifying and enjoining abstention from such available food.

What is absolutely certain is that such selections of diet and modifications of the physiological need are not biologically determined. Anybody who has had to look after a crawling or toddling child can bear witness that human infants are not born with instincts that enable them to distinguish the edible from the inedible, and reject the latter, much less distinguish between the approved and disapproved edible foods. The child has to

learn which foods it may eat; to an extent which sur-
prises many people, it also has to *learn* which foods to
enjoy.

In England or the United States we are so accustomed
to children preferring sweet foods, and being rewarded
with puddings, ice-cream, and candies, that we tend to
think of a childish preference for sweet things as
'natural'. This is, of course, not so; sugar has only been
available in sufficient quantities in the Occident for such
a taste to be generally developed in the last century or
so; and even where sugar is plentiful, it does not follow
that children prefer sweetened foods. Belgian mothers
have told me that they have more difficulty in getting
their children to eat the desserts than any other part of
the meal; Greek mothers do not understand that children
should be expected to like one part of a meal more than
another. In French North Africa one can see toddlers
happily chewing on raw red peppers which would bring
tears to the eyes of an unaccustomed European adult.

It is possible to note in any instance how and when
dietetic preferences and avoidances are inculcated, and
when they are so firmly established that children no
longer question them but regard them as 'human nature', and would be disgusted by food other than that to
which they have been habituated.[1]

Once these preferences have been established, the
search for their gratification may have the most far-
reaching economic, political, and military consequences.
The European conquest of much of Asia, with its con-

[1] See *National Research Council Bulletins*, 108 and 111, Washington,
D.C.

comitant wars and rivalries, had, as one of its chief motives, control of the spice trade; and spices were important and profitable because the European upper classes and the peoples of the Near East found unappetizing the monotonous diet which satisfied the greater number of the inhabitants of the temperate regions.

The social patterning of food preferences and avoidances does not of course deny the existence of individual preferences and avoidances within the range offered by a given society at a given time, nor even some individual shading between the accepted and rejected. A few English people learn to enjoy eating snails, and a few refuse to eat roast beef; but the English diet can be described and calculated with sufficient precision to guide the activities of large groups of people who may never have seen an Englishman eating, and who may have quite different preferences and avoidances themselves.

The transformation of physiological hunger into cultural appetite is a particularly concrete and easily verifiable illustration of the way in which all human physiological and emotional needs are patterned and modified by culture. It is, of course, much easier to demonstrate how hunger is patterned, restricted, and gratified, than to demonstrate how love or hate is patterned, restricted, and gratified, for the latter can only be shown indirectly and by inference through the prolonged observation of many variables.

All societies wish for 'freedom from want'—hunger and thirst—but each society has its idiosyncratic preferences as to the means by which its want should be alleviated; though it is true that some liberal but insular

authoritarian people think they should be made to alle-
viate their want in the way which is 'best' for them—a
quart of milk a day, for example. In the same way all
societies wish for 'freedom from fear', that is to say,
protection from internal and external dangers and op-
pressive interference; but in concrete instances this appears to have as many cultural variations as does the
alleviation of want. Each society, and by this I mean the
members of each society, seems to differ in what it considers the optimum of internal authority, and the demands it makes and the expectations it has from the
institutions of political authority and the people who are
in the positions of power. Each society too seems to
interpret in an idiosyncratic way the behaviour of foreign
countries and to ascribe different roles to them. Many
international misunderstandings would appear to arise
from the fact that each society tends to interpret the behaviour of its neighbours as though they were actuated
by the same needs and motives as the interpreter would
be if he acted in the same way; and this assumption
would appear to be often unjustified. There seems to be
no inherent reason why these political expectations and
demands should not be studied and analysed in the same
way as, say, economic demands.

2

Whenever a society is studied from the point of view
of analysing the predominant motives of its members, it
has been possible to demonstrate—or, perhaps more

exactly, to suggest with great plausibility—the means by
which the newborn infants are transformed into adult
members of their society, with—in the great majority of
cases—the wishes, the beliefs, and the habits common to
members of that society. Giving the word its fullest ex-
tension, the human infant is transformed into a member
of a specific society by education; but education, as here
used, means much more than formal instruction; it
means all the habits which are inculcated, whether consciously or not, and whether verbalized or not, from
birth onwards.

Intricate and elaborate experiments with animals have
confirmed the hypotheses advanced by Freud (among
others) of the preponderating importance of early learning.[1] Learning probably never stops, but the increment
of new learning, the rate of growth in the strength of
new habits, steadily decreases with repetition. It is for
this reason that the experiences of early life have such an
(apparently) disproportionate effect on later development.

In the life of the individual the development of specific
motives through appropriate education precedes the
manifestation of these motives in adult behaviour; but
this should not be interpreted to mean that, for the
society as a whole, these techniques of education are the
cause of the adult behaviour, far less to imply that the
transformation of specific items of education would result in a quick or automatic transformation of adult behaviour. Individuals have a childhood, but society does

---

[1] In technical mathematical language, learning tends to follow a
'growth curve'.

not. It is possible to describe with a certain degree of accuracy the devices which a particular society employs to educate the young so that they can replace the adults; but this does not imply that there are not alternative devices to produce the same ends. We still know very little of the effects of consciously imposed social control.

In description it is almost inevitable that only one aspect of this education can be discussed at a time, but this is purely a device of exposition. It should never be forgotten that the different experiences described in sequence are often undergone simultaneously, or nearly so, by the individual; and as a consequence it is not the individual items, but the pattern and sequence of these items, which constitute the idiosyncratic education which characterizes a given society. As far as we know, there are no items of behaviour or experience which are unique to one society; as far as we know, the pattern and sequence of items, in their entirety, are all unique to specific societies.

3

This book is not founded on my own experience and observation. I made two short Intourist visits to the U.S.S.R. in 1932 and 1936; but these are not good auspices for detailed research, even if—as was not the case —I had been scientifically equipped to take advantage of what I was able to see. My Russian was—and remains— rudimentary, enough to puzzle through a simple text with the aid of a dictionary. I have attempted to interpret and analyse the experience and observation of others.

In 1947 the late Professor Ruth Benedict, of Columbia University, organized the Columbia University Research Project on Contemporary Cultures, and invited me to participate in it. The project was organized to use immigrants, refugees, and those temporarily resident in the U.S.A., as informants on countries that were not immediately accessible to field work, with France as a control. The work of the project has since been described and illustrated in *The Study of Culture at a Distance*, edited by Margaret Mead and Rhoda Métraux (University of Chicago Press, 1953), which should be consulted for fuller details. I was invited to be the convener of the Russian group.

I was lucky in having a number of able collaborators in this work.[1] Nearly all of them had considerable training and knowledge in anthropology, psychology, and the other social sciences; many of them had long experience with Russia, and some of them had been born and reared in that country. We would meet at regular intervals to discuss the new material we had collected and to outline and clarify hypotheses deriving from this material, and to determine where confirmatory evidence might be found.

When I left England I had no clearly formulated ideas nor any knowledge of nor material on the Russians, save the recollections of my two short trips, vague memories of many Russian books and plays, and such

[1] They included Dr. Sula Benet, Dr. Margaret Mead, Dr. B. Schaffner, Dr. I. Telberg, Miss R. Zoglin, Dr. N. Leites, and Dr. M. Wolfenstein. Mrs. N. Hoyt, Mr. and Mrs. N. Calas, Miss M. Markovitz, and Mrs. S. Viton also gave help.

knowledge of recent Russian history as is common to most well-informed Englishmen of my generation.[1] So as to avoid arriving completely empty-handed, as well as empty-minded, I had the (I still think) brilliant idea of asking my friend John Rickman if I might take with me copies of the articles which he had contributed in 1938 to the *Lancet*, under the pseudonym of 'Vratch', concerning his experiences as a country doctor with the Friends' Relief in South Russia between 1916 and 1918.

Since these articles, together with other material never printed before, constitute the first part of this book, it would be unsuitable for me to expatiate here on their many qualities. It may be of interest, however, to describe the way in which these were used as a basis for discussion and a starting-point for research.[2]

The incident called here 'The Apology'—the story of the drunken peasant who tried to assault Dr. Rickman, and subsequently brought a formal apology witnessed by the village elders—was typed out and handed to the members of the group without any indication of its origin.

The first reaction of the Russian members of the group was that they felt there was something 'wrong' about the story. It took some discussion to elicit precisions as to what was 'wrong'; it wasn't the behaviour

---

[1] I did leave with one prejudice, which it may be interesting to record. I disagreed strongly with those people who claimed that the Russians were not Europeans; I thought they were echoing Dr. Goebbels's propaganda line.

[2] For those who are interested in the techniques of research, I have attempted to outline in Appendix I the means by which some of the major hypotheses in this study were arrived at.

of the peasants, perhaps it was the doctor not acting according to his status, not acting as a superior and learned man should act when confronted with his inferiors. I then explained that the doctor was a foreigner, an Englishman; and with this explanation the incident became, for the Russian members, completely understandable. One of the Russians said: 'I ought to have known that it was a foreigner; no Russian would kick a man who was standing up.'[1] It then developed that it was felt to be completely un-Russian to kick a standing man: you can knock a man over with your fist and then, if you are still angry, kick him when he is lying on the ground; but to kick a standing man is, for Russians, unthinkable. Subsequent interviewing showed that this feeling is very generally held; I could neither elicit explanations for it, nor was I able to fit it into any constructs I subsequently made. Consequently this note joins a number of other observations of behaviour and attitudes which seem to be specifically Russian but which find no place in a study as short and concentrated as this.

With this difficulty out of the way, we then discussed the specifically Russian behaviour described: the assumption by the elders of moral responsibility (? guilt) for the action of one of their co-villagers in which they had not participated in any way and of which they were not aware till after the occurrence; the insistence on the sincerity of the drunkard's repentance, and the manner

[1] In the text, the drunkard was not kicked, but pushed into a snowdrift by a push from the narrator's foot in his belly. This misinterpretation is, however, indicative in itself; and Great Russians do not seem to make much distinction between a kick and a push with the foot or leg.

of evoking and testing it; the formality of the apology, and how the doctor responded to it, and how a Russian would probably have responded. Discussion quickly developed a first list of unpleasant emotional states recognized by Russians and identified by different words, and an outline of the type of behaviour which would free one of the unpleasant feelings. This preliminary list gave a series of points to be explored in future interviews.

One of the Russians described the behaviour of the peasant as 'un-guilting' himself, a concept which could only very roughly be translated into conventional English. It was felt that this behaviour could be considered 'typically' Russian, and it was decided that it would be useful to collect and analyse other examples of 'un-guilting'. One member of the group undertook to analyse and excerpt the major novels of Dostoievsky and other Russian writers to discover other examples (there are, of course, a great many); another undertook to re-analyse the accounts of the purge trials of 1936 and after from the same point of view. Another relevant point to be investigated was the attitude of the Greek Orthodox Church towards guilt, confession and absolution; informants were to be interviewed on the subject, an attempt was to be made to interview one or more Orthodox priests, books on ritual were to be consulted. Another member of the group recalled a tale by Leskov which gave a very vivid description of the 'un-guilting' of a merchant, and undertook to translate it for us. The result of this series of investigations is subsumed later in this book.

It would of course, at least in theory, have been

possible to undertake all these researches without the stimulus of 'Vratch's' experience; but it seems—at any rate, to me—unlikely that we should have developed such a battery of relevant and co-ordinated work under other circumstances.

4

This summary account of one session of our group indicates the types of evidence from which the conclusions are drawn. They can be divided into interviews on the one hand, and documentary evidence on the other. There were no groups or colonies of Great Russians in the United States suitable for participant observation. The groups described as Russians in the census turned out to be chiefly Carpatho-Ukrainians (apart from the Jews of Russian origin, who were studied by another group in the project).

I did a considerable amount of the interviewing myself; but I was limited in my informants to the extent that I could only interview Russians who spoke English, French or German adequately. Interviews with interpreters were not successful. With a single exception, all my Russian informants were born members of the Orthodox Church and had lived at least till their adolescence in Great Russia. Many of my informants had reached adolescence before 1917, and had therefore grown up under the Imperial régime; the younger informants who had grown up under the Soviets were, however, of exceptional calibre.

Besides Russians, I interviewed a considerable number of non-Russians who had had good opportunities of observing Russian behaviour in recent years. These informants included journalists, government officials and their wives, businessmen, UNRAA officials, people who had lived in Eastern Germany during the Russian conquest and occupation, UNO officials, people who had studied Russian prisoners of war (forcibly enrolled in the German army or Todt organization), and the like. It was possible to have certain questions asked of a number of Russian 'displaced persons'. I regret that discretion makes it impossible to identify any of my informants by name, and to thank them publicly for their great assistance. In all, I have had access to between 300 and 400 interviews. About ten per cent of these were with technically qualified informants, who could give precise knowledge on some aspects of the lives of very many Russians. Many of these latter were interviewed several times. I have also had the benefit of John Rickman's detailed knowledge.

With two exceptions, the use of documentary evidence was not systematic; when subjects arose from the analysis of interviews and discussion on which further evidence was considered desirable, recourse was had to the excerpting and analysis of what seemed the most suitable books. Books on certain subjects which previous anthropological experience suggested would be illuminating, such as the organization of the village commune (*mir*) and folk-tales, were read with care. The two subjects on which the use of documentary material was systematic were the number and composition of the intelligentsia, and current and recent Soviet practices in child-rearing and education. Mrs. N. Hoyt undertook a very thorough study of the history of the intelligentsia, using all the available sources, ranging from the Russian census to memoirs, to assemble the available data about this most influential segment of Russian society;[1] and Dr. Margaret Mead supervised the analysis of all the recent and available brochures and text-books on child-rearing and pedagogy, including the analysis of several hundred photographs of children in crèches and state nurseries, courteously made available by the Soviet Photo Service in New York.

Because of the unsystematic use of documentary evidence I am not including a list of the books consulted from which no direct quotation is made.

This study is confined exclusively to the people of Great Russia, inhabiting that area of Russia corresponding to the Soviet Great Russian Republic and having Russian as their mother-tongue. At the time of the last Soviet census they represented about half the population of the U.S.S.R. In modern states the cultural and political boundaries frequently do not coincide; the multi-national character of the U.S.S.R. recognizes this fact explicitly.

Although on occasion to avoid clumsiness I have used the word 'Russian' without the prefix 'Great', no statement hereafter should be taken as applying to any group other than the Great Russians. I have not made myself —nor, as far as I know, has anyone else—studies comparable to this one on the peoples neighbouring the

[1] This material is not used to any extent in the present study.

Great Russians. It may, however, be of interest to state my present (very tentative) hypotheses about the relation of these neighbouring societies to the Great Russians, founded on spot interviewing and reading. For the peoples to the north-west and south-west, the White Russians and Ukrainians, it appears that there is no dramatic change, no 'cultural frontier', as it were, but a gradual modification of customs and attitudes which in turn merge into those of the Baltic states and Poland respectively. In contrast with this, there seems to be a sharply delimited 'cultural frontier' to the south and south-east, the Cossacks and the various peoples of the Caucasus, a contrast marked by differences of language, of social organization, and in some cases of religion.

This study is concerned exclusively with the Great Russians, and only with a single aspect of that very complex subject, their psychology, the shared motives and views of the world which appear to be predominant among them, and which cannot be reduced to the simple biological needs for food, shelter, warmth, and so on. The fact that I do not discuss, except incidentally, such subjects as their history, their economics, their contemporary social and political organization and the like should not be interpreted to mean that I do not consider these subjects to be of the greatest importance for a complete picture. I do not discuss them because I do not feel myself competent to discuss them; I lack the knowledge and special training which would enable me to contribute constructively to the discussion of these aspects of human society; I cannot do more than accept the statements of recognized experts, and repeat them when they are essential to my argument. It is my hope that studies of national character, such as the one which follows, may illuminate some of the problems developed by history, economics, and political science, and suggest new subjects of research and different techniques of gathering and interpreting their data to the practitioners of these sciences and arts.

5

I have made this study with the greatest objectivity of which I am capable, but it is almost impossible to-day for a person to be without some personal bias concerning Soviet Russia. After some hesitation—for it exposes me as having followed fairly closely the intellectual trends then fashionable—I have decided that it is fair to my readers to outline in summary detail the vagaries of my biases on this subject.

I do not think I had any very definite attitudes towards Russia before my first visit there in 1932. I returned from this visit enthusiastic for the country and the régime. Nobody I think can come into personal contact with the ordinary unofficial Russians without being deeply attracted by their warmth, their sincerity, their apparent lack of anxiety, and their enthusiasm. This was the period of mass unemployment, confusion, and despair in England and Germany (which was on our way to the U.S.S.R.); despite the evidence of very great poverty nearly everywhere in the U.S.S.R., the general enthusiasm and confidence in the future were almost intoxicating. At that period no bars were placed on the contact between foreigners and Russians, or at least, none that one could notice; provided some sort of common language could be found, Russian friendliness and hospitality were given free rein.

Between this visit and my return in 1936 my enthusiasm and partisanship increased. The spirited defence of Dimitrov at the Reichstag fire trial, the firm Soviet opposition to fascism and national-socialism as compared with our half-hearted flirtations with these monstrous tyrannies, Litvinov's unequivocal behaviour at the League of Nations contrasted sharply with the brutality and misery of the means test and hunger marches at home, and our dishonourable foreign policy. In a book which I wrote in 1935 (a good part of which was occupied with making fun of our local communists) I described myself as a 'pink' and 'a fellow-traveller'. We were political innocents in those days, and such terms were then little more than expressions of sympathy.

The material improvement in Leningrad and Moscow between 1932 and 1936 was striking; but although our visit was before the big purge trials and the subsequent xenophobia, the atmosphere seemed to me much less exhilarating. The contrasts between rich and poor, between over-privileged and under-privileged, were far more marked than they had been earlier; communist party members had been released from their earlier quasi-Franciscan vows of poverty; the food provided in the different-class canteens and restaurants varied as much in quantity and quality as in any parallel capitalist organizations.

My enthusiasm rose again with the positive Russian

action in the Spanish civil war, as contrasted with our own equivocation; but it was severely deflated by George Orwell's account of his experiences in Catalonia, and by the reading of André Gide's *Retour de l'U.R.S.S.* and Franz Borkenau's *Third International*. I subsided into a non-political emotional indifference, from which I was shocked by the Molotov-Ribbentrop agreement. While not more 'immoral' than the Munich agreement, it destroyed completely the Soviet claims to ethical superiority.

Although most thankful for the valiant fighting qualities of the Russian army, I did not wholly share the general enthusiasm for our gallant ally, for my war-work forced my attention on their very dubious behaviour, first in Iran and subsequently in South-East Europe. By the end of the war, I considered that communism was a tyranny nearly as evil as national-socialism; I made in my own mind an explicit distinction between communists and Russians.

The final change, to date, in my bias concerning the Soviet Union occurred during the investigations on which this study is based. It seemed to me that what I had formerly described as communist could more properly be described as Russian; the continuities between Czarist and Soviet Russia appeared most striking; the contrasts, where they existed, between pre- and post-revolutionary Russia seemed like the contrasts between mirror images, or algebraical statements in which only the sign has been altered. I re-read some of Lenin as a document on Russian character; a re-reading of earlier visitors to Muscovy, especially perhaps the Marquis de Custine, seemed to confirm this belief.

This then is my bias to-day. I consider that Russia, or rather the Russian government, is an expanding prose-lytizing force with a system of values and methods of imposing them which shock and revolt me, and which stand in opposition to the values and methods which we honour in theory, however much we may betray them in practice. As such, Russia and its government are a potential danger to our values and our security; but this potential danger will only become actual if our weakness, our inconsistency or our mismanagement of our own affairs make us appear an inevitable prey. I think war is more likely to come through mistakes and mis-understandings than through evil intent on either side. In an attempt to lessen the occasions for unnecessary misunderstandings and misinterpretations, I am pub-lishing this preliminary study of Russian psychology, though I am well aware of its many deficiencies and ten-tative character. The field is a new one; and I hope that this first foray will be followed by stronger forces, that this sketch-map will be amended and completed by an army of cartographers. It is an attempt to remove the sign 'terra incognita' from an important area of our political maps.

GEOFFREY GORER

Somerset,
  January 1949

INTRODUCTION—1961

THIS BOOK was the forerunner of a series of studies of
the people of Soviet Russia employing anthropological
and psychological concepts (rather than political, military, or economic data) as a technique for increasing
our understanding of the implicit values and assumptions which underlie the overt behaviour of the peoples
of the U.S.S.R. and their leaders. Among the books
produced by my colleagues in the Russian group of
Columbia University's Research in Contemporary Cultures and its successor, mention must be made of
Margaret Mead's *Soviet Attitudes toward Authority*
(McGraw-Hill, 1951); Nathan Leites' *The Opera-
tional Code of the Politburo* (McGraw-Hill, 1951);
Nathan Leites' and Elsa Bernaut's *Ritual of Liquidation*
(Free Press, 1954); H. S. Dinerstein's *Communism
and the Russian Peasant* (Free Press, 1955); L. Haim-
son's *The Russian Marxist and the Origin of Bolshevism*
(Harvard University Press, 1955); the relevant sections
of *The Study of Culture at a Distance,* edited by Mar-
garet Mead and Rhoda Métraux (University of Chicago
Press, 1953). This last item contains a very full bibliography of relevant studies published up to that date.
Sections of *Childhood in Contemporary Cultures,*
edited by Margaret Mead and Martha Wolfenstein
(University of Chicago Press, 1955) deal specifically

with contemporary child-training ideals in the U.S.S.R.

Nearly contemporary with the R.C.C. studies sponsored by Columbia University and the Rand studies sponsored by the American Museum of Natural History was the Harvard Project on the Soviet Social System, under the direction of the late Professor Clyde Kluckhohn. A great number of specialized publications have come out of this project; they are mostly subsumed in *How the Soviet System Works* by Bauer, Inkeles and Kluckhohn (Harvard University Press, 1956); and *The Soviet Citizen* by Alex Inkeles and others (Harvard University Press, 1959). It was under the auspices of the Harvard University Research Center that Dr. H. V. Dicks intensively interviewed a considerable number of Soviet defectors and refugees in Germany (reported in his *Observations on Contemporary Russian Behaviour,* Human Relations Vol. V, No. 2, 1952), arriving at very similar conclusions to those outlined in this book.

Besides these studies which were influenced by anthropological and psychological concepts, there is a continuous stream of books on the U.S.S.R. of every level of accuracy and scholarship from the most refined to the most journalistic, a stream so great that it is almost a full-time occupation to keep abreast of the literature. When I finished this book in 1949 I expressed the wish that 'this first foray will be followed by stronger forces, that this sketch-map will be amended and completed by an army of cartographers.' On one level, at least, this wish has been granted; but, as in the tradition of fairy stories, the granting of the wish has not altogether produced the effects wished for. There are now available infinitely more facts and judgments about the people and institutions of the U.S.S.R than there were in 1948; but it is, to say the least, questionable whether the attitudes of informed people and political leaders in the Western world towards the U.S.S.R. are more rational than they were when this book was written. And the development of rational attitudes—knowledge instead of prejudice, understanding instead of fear, humanism instead of diabolism (if the proper implication of these terms be allowed)—has been the major object of nearly all the books which have been written about the peoples and institutions of the U.S.S.R. It was quite explicitly my aim, and that of my esteemed collaborator, the late John Rickman, in publishing this book.

2

It would be disingenuous of me not to acknowledge that this book attained a certain notoriety, far beyond its readership, because of its introduction of the swaddling hypotheses and because of the wide-spread imputation that I affirmed that swaddling was 'the cause' of the Great Russian character, with the further implication that changing this item of infant care would by itself modify the character of Great Russians. On the factual level this is simply untrue; it is explicitly rejected in several portions of the text (pp. 8, 128–9, 198). But the fact that this rumour has had so wide a diffusion is itself of interest; and it seems worth de-

voting a little space to considering the possible reasons
for this.

In a brilliant paper in the *American Anthropologist*
(Vol. 56, No. 3, 1954), entitled 'The Swaddling Hypothesis: Its Reception,' Margaret Mead outlined with
great clarity some of the reasons for the naive confusion
between studies (such as this) which try to discover how
a newborn infant becomes a fully participating member
of his own culture and society and historical studies
of the origins of a society and its component institutions. She gives the example of language. It is perfectly
possible to study in great detail how an infant learns
to speak its own language, be it French or Russian or
Thai, without implying any theory about the origin
of the language learned, or the origin of languages in
general. A description of the process by which individuals learn is not a history of the origins of what is
learned. She also deals in some detail with the political
motives which led some groups to attack and misrepresent these hypotheses with extraordinary persistence.

In the light of experience, however, I recognize that
I am somewhat to blame for the confusion. Not that
I think the facts are wrong: indeed, further information has confirmed nearly all the material about the
treatment of infants [1] and young children which I
adduced. Where I made a mistake was the order in

---

[1] One of the most striking of these confirmations was an account given by
the daughter of the Indian Ambassador to the U.S.S.R. of her delivery in a
Moscow hospital, and the way she was taught to treat her baby by the nurses
and pediatricians there. From her account we learn—a fact not reported earlier
—that very young babies cry to have the swaddling replaced. (*The Birth of a
Baby—Moscow Style*, by Parvathi Thampi. *New York Times Magazine*, May
20, 1956, page 19ff.)

which I presented the data: if I had presented the data on adults before the chapters on children, portraying adult characteristics before I dealt with the antecedent early learning, I think there might have been less cause, or at least less excuse, for confusion. The reader may, if he will, make the experiment of reading Chapters III and IV of the section, *The Psychology of Great Russians,* before he reads Chapters I and II. With this simple transposition, at least one cause of confusion might have been avoided.

To my disappointment, there have not been, as far as I know, any consistent psychological or psychoanalytic studies of the hypotheses advanced in this book; we have no further information to confirm or deny the effects on future development of restriction of hand-mouth exploration, of grasping, or of movements of the limbs, and so on, in the first months of life. The swaddling hypotheses are still hypotheses.

3

Although from the theoretical point of view the swaddling hypotheses are the most novel features, with implications for psychodynamics and social anthropology, this book was not written with the intention of giving them prominence. From my point of view, the nub of the book, the section by which it stands or falls, is Chapter V, *Conclusions,* and above all the ten political maxims on pp. 191–94. The rest of the book, as far as my contribution is concerned (I think John Rickman's *Russian Camera Obscura* has permanent literary value and is worthy of comparison with the sketches of Turgeniev), can and should be read as documenting the ways in which and the evidence through which I derived these maxims. But the maxims themselves are not dependent on their derivation. They can be tested against Soviet behaviour today, or at any time in the immediate past, as it has been reported in all the different media of communication; and I make bold to claim that, by such tests, the maxims stand up to the history of recent years quite adequately, and can still, I think, give guidance to international relations with the U.S.S.R. and help in achieving a tolerable and durable *modus vivendi* between the West and the Soviets which will avoid the unimaginable disaster of a thermonuclear war.

I think, however, that some of these maxims are too condensed; and it may be useful to elaborate one or two of them, in particular the implication of the term *strength* in maxims (v) and (x). These read:

(v) The analogy of the dike describes the only type of political behaviour which will contain Russian expansion: firmness, strength, consistency. And the greatest of these is consistency.

(x) The one situation which might evoke war (apart from the Western powers 'compressing' Russia) would be if the Western Powers manifested such weakness, or such alternations between strength and weakness, that the Russians would feel compelled to advance to such a degree that the Western powers would feel that the menace was intolerable.

'Strength' in these contexts is not a synonym for 'military might', any more than 'consistency' is a synonym for 'obstinacy'. In the contemporary world, an appropriate amount of armaments is a component of strength, but strength cannot be reduced to a counting of lethal hardware and manpower in the forces. It is fortunate for us that this is the case; for, under present conditions, an authoritarian government in peacetime can always divert a greater proportion of its resources and manpower to military ends than can a democracy; were strength so simply defined, it would be well-nigh impossible for us to match the Russians over years.

Nor is strength manifested by threats, by rocket-rattling, or by minor provocative actions. Here again, were this the case, we would be outmatched. With their conviction of being in the Truth, of being justified by history in all their acts, the Russians can much more easily act in defiance of articulate world opinion (as was shown by their series of nuclear tests in October and November, 1961) than the governments of the West can or will ever be able to do while they honour any of the principles of democracy. We cannot, and by our standards we certainly should not, try to rival the Soviets in actions which, while they might strike fear in opponents, certainly do frighten and distress large and articulate sections of our own populations and of much of the rest of the world. The Russians can tolerate hate and fear which they have knowingly provoked with far less distress than we are able to do. We—the Americans perhaps even more than the British —are dependent for our self-respect on the feeling that the rest of the world respects and likes us; the

Great Russians are sure that the rest of the world is 'objectively' hostile ('At least today Russians do not admit of neutrality: he who is not completely for them is "objectively" hostile, however friendly his overt feelings and behaviours.' p. 161). Therefore they feel few qualms in affronting other peoples' hopes or fears. A 'policy of strength' is, luckily, not synonymous with rocket-rattling or 'brinkmanship'; were it so, our chances would be poor. I think it is quite certain that with displays of 'brinkmanship' we frighten ourselves far more than we frighten the Russians; the individual Great Russian is likely to have far less free-floating anxiety than the individual Westerner (in the colloquial phrase, they have 'steadier nerves') and, as is pointed out in maxim (vi), they find the strategical retreat a highly acceptable manoeuvre. It is pointless to play 'chicken' unless both parties accept the same definitions of the ways in which courage or fear are shown. For the Great Russians a temporary retreat is not a humiliation.

Military power is only one of the implications of 'strength', according to my intention in the maxims quoted above. Consider the implications of 'strong-minded', 'strong-willed', a 'strong head', a 'strong faith', 'strength of character', and similar phrases in common use; these, I think, indicate the type of strength we need if we are to live with (rather than die with) the Soviet Russians. Above all, we need the strength of our convictions; and we permanently diminish our strength if, for the sake of a momentary advantage, we act in a way which affronts our strong consciences.

The greatest apparent threat to our moral strength is that we shall be seduced by overt fear and hidden admiration of the Communist system into copying those features of their system which are alien to our strongest-held values: free-floating suspicion, imputing guilt by intention or association, attempting to impose a formalized ideology, fear of heterodoxy.

Our moral strength, our strength of purpose are as important to us in dealing with the Russians as is our military strength. Not more important: 'My strength is as the strength of ten, because my heart is pure' is, unfortunately, only metaphorically true. But if our heart is not pure, if we sacrifice our moral principles for the sake of expediency or try to engage in a contest of amoral Machiavellism with the Russians, then our strength will be correspondingly diminished. If we are not to annihilate one another, we can look forward to a life-time of negociations; and in negociations, strength of purpose is of comparable importance to strength of arms.

Strength of purpose is not the same thing as obstinacy and stand-patness. It is foolish to assume that the state of the world is perfect, that any change is a change for the worse; or that there is automatic virtue in opposing any proposal that the Soviets may make. To believe that a willingness to negociate is a sign of weakness, that in negociations we have everything to lose and nothing to gain, is a mark of despair; it is the opposite face of that panic of submission—'it's better to be red than dead'—which—when it is honest, and not merely a mask of communism—betrays an equal lack of confidence in the values to which we at least pay lip service, an equal lack of moral strength.

In any situation, other than a demand for unconditional surrender, there are some elements which are negociable without the betrayal of moral principle and others which are not. Once these discriminations have been made, their maintenance is a test of strength of purpose. Great Russian negociators are not likely to make the same discriminations, even as an intelligence exercise, and will quite certainly try to get the maximum advantage at every point. When they finally recognize the strength of purpose with which some positions are maintained, particularly if there is consistency with which the positions are held from one context to another and from one set of negociations to another, there is every reason to suppose that they will withdraw their more extreme demands and reach a perfectly tolerable modus vivendi. The election of U Thant to replace Mr. Hammarskjold as Secretary General of the United Nations in November 1961, after the very persistent Soviet attempt to have the Secretary General replaced by a troika, is a good, recent example of this process. In our somewhat atomistic short-term view of historical events, we may interpret this outcome as a 'defeat' for the Russians, since they gave up their previous demands. I do not think that the Russians see the situation in this way. They had gone to the limits of their strength in pushing their demands as strongly as they could. When they came up against the moral strength of those people and countries who would not allow the position of the Secretary General to be compromised, they made one more strategic retreat.

4

It may be thought that the last few pages have passed the boundaries proper to a social anthropologist; but I would maintain that they only make explicit ideas latent in the maxims of Chapter V, and that these maxims are directly derived from the evidence presented in the previous chapters. It seems to me inevitable that the study of the national characters of contemporary societies should result in maxims or generalizations which have political implications. Indeed, did they not have this result there would be little reason for accepting the difficulties of studying large and heterogeneous societies rather than the smaller and less differentiated 'primitive' societies which are our traditional field of work.

If we accept the fact that all the peoples of the world are human, with the same physiology and the same psychological potentialities, whatever their present level of technological development, system of values, or political organization, and that all human beings are organized into societies with distinctive cultures, then all human beings and human societies can be studied, at least potentially, by the scientific techniques which have been developed to these ends. Of these scientific techniques, social anthropology and whole-person psychology (including depth psychology and the developing data of ethology) are the most appropriate. Psychology has shown that in the life of any individual the process of learning is cumulative, so that earlier learning influences later learning; social anthropology has shown that culture is continuous over more than one generation, that the people who die are replaced by new members who have learned, by both conscious and unconscious processes, the values and customs appropriate to their culture and their position in it, or, in other words, their individual variation of the national character. This national character is susceptible to scientific study.

Whether or no there is articulate knowledge of the national characters of the representatives involved in international negociations at any level, this factor of national character must play a continuous and influential role. Even on the most superficial level of vocabulary, there is little likelihood that abstract terms such as 'freedom', 'democracy', 'free elections', 'self-determination', 'compromise', will have identical referents for representatives of different societies, even when they have similar political forms and use variants of the same language. When political forms, levels of technology, and language are markedly different, it is quite certain that the words, and the values concealed therein, have different referents; and, unless this is explicitly realized, any agreement is likely to be shortly followed by charges of bad faith in the fulfilment of the agreement reached. All parties to the agreement are likely to feel that the others have failed in their undertakings, while they themselves have acted most loyally.

Today I believe that the only major risk of major war lies in exacerbated mutual misunderstandings. Though both the U.S.S.R. and the U.S.A. have groups who consider the other society so abominable, so divorced from common humanity, that the proper course is to destroy it forthwith, I think there is little likelihood of either of these groups of fanatics—the 'anti-party' group in the U.S.S.R. or the ephemeral right-wing anti-communist groups in the U.S.A. momentarily typified by the John Birch society—achieving political power; though it is possible that the internal necessity to placate these groups may lead the existing governments to displays of 'toughness' which incidentally exacerbate the tensions of the international scene. But genuine misunderstandings seem to me the real risk. It is in the hope that, at least to some degree, this book may diminish causes for misunderstanding, that I present it again to the public.

Sunte House,   G.G.
Haywards Heath
    November, 1961

Russian Camera Obscura
Ten Sketches of Russian Peasant Life (1916–1918)

BY JOHN RICKMAN

NOTE: *On my return from Russia, where I was a country doctor with the Friends' War Victims Relief Unit between* 1916 *and* 1918, *the Editor of* The Atlantic Monthly *asked me for some articles. The sketches here called* 'Peasant Officers' *and* 'Police' (*and slightly revised and abbreviated*) *appeared in* 1919 *in that magazine under other titles.*

In 1937 *the Editor of* The Lancet *asked me for four articles to appear, under a pseudonym, in his column* 'Grains and Scruples'. *They were to be a bit medical, about Russia but only mildly political, and to have journalistic interest. I wrote about a dozen which I named* 'Russian Camera Obscura', *and from among these he chose the four here entitled* 'The Apology', 'The Threat', 'Snow', *and* 'Moujiks want Glasses', *all of which appeared in* The Lancet *in* 1938 *under the pseudonym* 'Vratch', *which is the Russian for Physician.*

IRON

THE PEASANTS were desperately poor and their standard of living was low. When the crops were bad they starved, when good they filled out again; but even a succession of good seasons did not raise them out of their sunken condition of endless struggle for the barest living. Four factors in about equal degree united to keep them down. Their religion told them that suffering was acceptable in God's sight, and their Church, which fattened on their offerings, made return by an education better in Old Church Slavonic than in modern Russian and arithmetic. Their Temporal Rulers, even more rapacious than their Spiritual, taxed the poor almost to starving-point while allowing the rich to go almost duty-free—a business error which the Church never makes. In addition the Czarist régime opposed initiative on the ground that it was conducive to revolution, so that an enterprising villager who went about picking up ideas, even though only on farming, was suspect.

A third factor was their ill health. Undernourishment and lack of drugs, ignorance of hygiene and the belief that illness was from God, kept them more inert than they should have been. At times they rose like giants to great feats of toil, but like sick people the world over, they had not the capacity for a sustained activity which at the same time called for initiative. They were not lazy, but their grasp of new ideas, a new technique, was slow and feeble; the external world did not seem to them to be theirs to master.

A fourth factor lay in the unwillingness of the villagers to allow competition among themselves; as members of a community they must all think alike and act alike. The sharing of almost every task encouraged a certain handiness at many crafts but discouraged the development of outstanding skill in any one. It was against the village spirit to compel respect for any achievement that all could not in fairly close degree emulate. Peasants in other parts of Russia had village industries, here there were none. Those who felt an itch to be doing more or better than their neighbours found their way to the towns, returning for the harvests, and going their ways when country duties were over.

*   *   *   *   *

Here follows a small piece of amateurish 'field work', as anthropologists might call it which though not strictly medical, nevertheless could not easily have been carried out except by a doctor (or a priest) since no other persons had the privilege, accorded only to 'one of us', to enter the houses without knocking, and whose presence did not create a class-consciousness or sense of being Visited.

I set out to make a survey of the consumption of iron, and I will give at once my estimate of it in the poorest village that I visited, viz. about five pounds per head per generation! When I added the ounces up and divided by the number surviving in the village during the previous thirty years as near as one could estimate, that was the astonishing result. With this small consumption that community kept even in its struggle with nature. Through constant wear, loss by rust and burning away by heat, renewals of this (to them) most precious metal are needed from time to time. But iron is hard and elastic, it gives under strain and does not often snap, breakages were not common and such was the care lavished on the metal that very little was lost through carelessness and the consumption was due almost wholly to wear. When I add that on a rougher estimate but on the same basis, rather more than six hundred pounds of wood was used it will be seen how near the raw earth these people lived.

Let us watch a small house being built, all the time estimating the amount of material that goes into its construction and the durability of the product.

A peasant's hut of the poorest sort, if made on the steppe where you can drive all day without finding a stone large enough or hard enough to crack a brazil nut, will be fashioned out of clay and mud, puddled together by the feet of the girls, who fasten their skirts to knee-height and stamp and churn the slime to the accompaniment of songs until it reaches the right consistency, and then tread in straw as a binder, till the mixture binds on their feet, and however lusty they may be they can hardly move in it. It is a terrific labour and the wenches develop thighs of iron in the work, but it is a matter of pride to endure it. A girl of about seventeen came with a septic foot and begged me to get it healed quickly or she could not stand in with the rest. I told her she must not work her foot while the bandages were on, so sepsis or no she took the bandages off, and, confound it, she was no worse for it! I found out later that not only is it a matter of pride before those of her own age to endure a long day in the clay, but the mothers urge them to it as the work is said to improve their ardour in embrace and to strengthen them against the pains of childbed. I can well believe it.

The stiff clay and straw mixture is then laid out on a smoothed piece of level ground, patted to an even thickness and cut with the edge of a spade. The blocks are about nine inches thick by twelve by eighteen and the spade cuts are renewed during the first stage of drying.

As soon as the sun has taken off the first moisture from the upper surface, and the level ground (powdered with a carpet of fine earth or dust to the level of half an inch, much as a cook powders a pastry board) has absorbed some of the moisture from the underside, the blocks are raised with a spade and carried to a drying ground. They are here laid on their side and turned from time to time till they are hard and dry and crumble like biscuit if knocked or cut.

The ground for the house is cleared during this time and also puddled and left to dry out, care being taken to screen it from too much sun with wisps of straw. A trench is dug about six inches deep in the hardened soil and the sun-dried blocks laid in to a width of about two and a half feet. This is smeared with a stiffer mixture of clayey soil and the 'courses' run to a height of about two to three feet from the ground.

I was not able to note any special technique in the

binding of the blocks. Those that fitted nicely together were mated, an irregularity of spade cut matching another hump or hollow in a neighbouring block as near as may be. There were no hollows in the walls except such as came from careless laying of the blocks, and in the majority of instances no framework of wood; the walls were too heavy to need stiffening, and strong enough to carry the thatch and inner roof.

Except at the space for the door frame, the threshold being about a foot above ground, this thick wall is carried round the entire rectangle of the house; on this level windows will rest, but above this level the walls will be only eighteen inches thick, flush on the inside with the extra thickness without acting as an additional defence against the splash of raindrops from the thatch, and the sogging of melting snow.

At an inside height of about eight or nine feet, there will be laid a plate on the top of the wall near its outer margin. This is usually a pine tree with a sector cut off so that it lies flat. On this are laid the ceiling joists, and, notched into it, the foot of the rafters. These are left in the round, irregular in shape and meeting at the top, usually without a ridge plate, being notched and pegged together. As the roof will be thatched there will be enough lathing, tied and pegged to the rafters, to give lateral rigidity. The inner roof (it is more than a ceiling) is in the better houses boarded across from wall to wall; in the poorest it is a wattle and daub lashed under and another larger one lashed over the joists. On the top, above the ceiling and under the thatch—before the thatch is put on—is spread about four inches of sun-baked clay dust and earth. This acts as a non-conducting layer against heat and cold.

Now that we have got the walls up and the roof on let us see what tools have been used. A spade for the clay, an axe for felling the timber, a saw for cutting the planks for the ceiling if planked, an adze for smoothing out the plates and notching the rafters, and an auger for making the holes. The weight of wood is about one and a half tons. In this fourteen by eleven foot house a family can have a roof over them and live for generations at the cost of three sledge-hauls from the forest and so far not an ounce of iron.

Now for the stove. Its outside dimensions are six feet by four feet six and nearly five feet high. It is composed of two arches above one another, the upper one is the oven, the lower one is for ashes, pot hooks, fire-raker, and such-like apparatus. The bed of the oven, which is placed at a convenient height from the floor, is oval and is two feet six from back to front and two feet wide in the short diameter. The arched roof curves down at the back to the oven-bed, and at the front lips down a bit so that the fumes and heat of the fire do not go roaring up the chimney too fast. The flue does not go straight up to the roof but rises to the ceiling, turns horizontally, descends, and ascends again (or it may take another double bend) so that there is at least nine feet of flue to absorb the heat of the burning before the final flight through the chimney stack is made. The flue takes up rather over a foot in thickness and rests on another arch, so that anyone looking at the stove from in front would see the mouth of this small cavern at waist height flanked with the curving buttresses that support the flue, like the shallow porchway of a Norman church, with the narrower round-topped arch of the oven behind.

The height of the cavern from oven bed to domed roof is about fifteen inches, so the 'brickwork' at its thinnest at the top is a foot thick, and the same at the sides; but as the stove is almost a cube (with this tortoise-shaped hollow in the middle of it) the thrust from a weight on its level top is taken by the more massive 'brickwork' of the corners rather than that of the thinner sides. The weight on the top is of course Grandpapa. Here through the long days and longer nights he and Granny and perhaps a grandchild lie in warmth, covered by sheepskins, and reach down for food.

Of the under arch nothing much need be said, but the flue has a complication. In order that the heated bricks should not continue to draw up cool air, warm it, and waste it into the cold of winter, it is necessary to have a damper of some sort—a piece of sheet iron rather thicker than the side of a biscuit tin suffices.

When building this stove there are three places where iron is used. A strip a twelfth of an inch thick and an inch and a quarter wide bent to an arch, and plugged in at its feet to the bed of the oven, forms a margin to that lip of the cavern I spoke of which comes down and curbs the outrush of flames and heat from the fire within to the flue without. It serves a double function, it prevents the licking flames from burning away the sundried bricks quite so fast, and by its greater hardness and elasticity it takes better than would brick the knocks of pots carelessly inserted or withdrawn from the oven.

This piece of iron needs occasional renewing, say once every twenty years. That small strip is the first essential piece of iron in the structure of the house, and with the exception of the damper and the thin oven door, it is the last.

To use wood as fuel could only be compared for extravagance to burning one's Hepplewhite furniture. The fuel is dried manure. The farmyard droppings of the year are spread in a flat-topped circular heap and a few bucketfuls of water poured in the middle. The village girls then press it with their feet as they did the clay till it forms a smooth firm paste. Much the same procedure is adopted as with the clay except that less straw is used as a binder. The blocks are not more than four inches thick and six by nine in the other dimensions. These when thoroughly sun-dried are stacked in heaps seven feet high, tapering towards the top as peat is stacked in Ireland. This manure fuel behaves much like peat except that it has less 'life' in it but is better than the camels' dung which the Arabs burn in the desert. It makes a gritty ash from which it is hard to get a clean lye; accordingly the home-made soap obtained from boiling grease with the ash water is rough like sandstone.

*　　*　　*　　*　　*

Now a few details, for it is not yet a very habitable house. That thickening of the wall outside is, on the street side, usually made thicker still so as to form a seat. The stove is placed in a corner with a foot clearance all round so that no precious heat will be conducted away. Its mouth is near the doorway, because, I was told, if it should fume carbon monoxide the poison would soon blow away, and in this position there are fewer draughts across the room. The windows are never opened in winter, a film of water on a casement freezes the window frame as tight as glue. In summer one of the two eighteen by eighteen inch windows is opened or removed.

The door is heavily padded on the inside; a sheepskin stuffed with extra wool is stretched over it. It is held down with battens fastened usually with flat-headed nails, sometimes with wooden pegs. With these nails we finish the metal work of the house: the door swings on a peg of wood, fitting snug by leather-lined door jambs; the window hinges are of leather—ah, I forgot, a dozen tin-tacks to hold them on for the one window—if made to open. In sum: 3 sledge loads of wood, $1\frac{1}{2}$ tons; iron, 3 lb.; and a house that will last for three generations.

We will furnish the house: a wooden bed frame five feet six long and two feet six broad for both parents, a table thirty by forty-five inches, three benches fifteen inches wide (more generous than most) and five feet long on which the boys will sleep, a wider bench twenty inches wide and also five feet long for two of the girls, a chest three feet long and two wide at the head of the parents' bed and against the wall by the back of the stove. No one sleeps on this, partly because Gaffer steps on it when he gets down from the stove. If the family becomes more numerous further accommodation for huddled repose will be needed. A deep shelf may be slung at a height of two to three feet from the ceiling if this will bear the strain. This shelf is up to five feet from back to front and four or five feet wide. It is in the warm and fuggy zone of air at the top of the room, the worst-ventilated part of the chamber; well out of the way the younger children sleep here.

A certain degree of privacy is sometimes obtained by erecting a partition parallel with the parental bed; this reaches to the ceiling but as it only juts out from the wall the same length as the bed which is in full view of the three on the stove it can only be described as a partial privacy. I have seen a curtain from partition to wall en-closing the tiny bedroom in fewer than half a dozen such huts (and remember that I visited patients without knocking at all hours of the twenty-four; and when travelling burst in with equal lack of ceremony for a few hours' sleep on the floor if the night was too dark even for Russian horses to pick their way in safety). Such cur-taining was not considered decent; neither are the win-dows covered. Among adults I came across no prying —the children it was thought did not count. A child who peeped got his face smacked, but wasn't told not to do it again. He was slapped not for his good but be-cause the grown-up was annoyed. (To go on with this aspect of their sexual life, the women above puberty bathed in their shift, the men went naked but when out of the water covered the pudenda with a hand. In the vapour baths the men and women bathed at different times.)

Thus far the house itself is finished, but to prevent a heavy in-gust of air when the padded door is open there is always a large porch outside, built of those same blocks of clay and straw but with thinner walls. The thatched roof is carried on over it but there is no ceiling.

It has a wattle door and no windows. Add for this therefore three more hundredweight of wood but no more iron. The byres which are built round the small court or farmyard will of course need more wood (but no more iron) for their construction.

Now for the farm implements: the plough was made of wood with an iron tip to the share weighing less than two pounds, the coulter was usually made of wood, though occasionally edged with iron; the axles of the farm carts were of wood, sometimes with a thin metal strip an inch wide and five inches long laid on the top to take the weight; the wooden wheels were usually rimless and bumped at each revolution as the gap in the rim hit the ground; the harrows were wooden, and so of course were the runners of the sledges.

So if the farmstead is on the same scale as the house, for the structure of the entire farmstead and contents (including carts, sledges, ploughs and tools) we shall need: wood about six tons; iron about thirty-five pounds.

SNOW

O<small>NE</small> <small>EVENING</small> just after tea in the middle of winter, the servants in my hospital came to tell me that a peasant wished me to pay a visit. A snowstorm was blowing up so I knew the matter was serious. In the hall a dejected peasant was standing waiting. He asked if I would go to a woman who had been delivered four days before, but was desperately ill. When he told me it was his wife a chill struck us as if the felt-covered door had blown open and let in the cold air. We were accustomed to tragic news from those thus facing possible bereavement; but in addition these words conveyed to us the fact that the snowstorm now raging was so terrific that the poor fellow could not persuade any friend or relative to face it. Though she was dying he had had to leave his wife and himself risk even disaster in getting aid. I made only one stipulation, that after my work for his wife was done he must get me driven back for the hospital duties next morning. He agreed and we set out.

As a sensible person when rations are uncertain will stuff into himself as much as he can eat, to make up for depleted reserves and lay in a provision for the future, so any sensible traveller leaving a warm stove and wrapped in sheepskins, still warm from the cupboard, would snatch a period of sleep before the frost began to cause distress. By the time the sledge had reached the end of the village I was asleep. It was an uneventful twenty miles. The night was terribly cold but it did not break through my layers of fur. Innermost was a close-cropped sheepskin lining to a sort of melton greatcoat, outside of which was a coat of long-haired sheepskin, not buttoned but held together with tied thongs. Over all was a garment transcending tailors' terminology, shaped to be sure like a coat but so large that thirteen sheepskins had gone to its making. This vast envelope, showing to the world the white inside of the pelts, was kept in position by a girdle curiously patterned and woven in scarlet and white, half a yard wide and four or five yards long—a present from a grateful Tartar—wrapped round the belly of this mountain of hides. The collar when open fell over the shoulders like a mantle; when closed it crossed over the face and stood up like a conical dome over its wearer's head and was kept from falling by a narrow hand-woven braid tied in front with a bow knot for quick release in case of being pitched head-first into a snowdrift. The feet were protected with stockings made of camel hair, thick as blankets, and the legs were thrust into knee-high wide felt boots; there must be no pressure for if skin circulation is stopped even over a small area the result is frost-bite, and (since it may in the recoverable stage pass unnoticed) necrosis. It was indeed wise therefore to get one's sleep while one was still warm.

When I unpacked the instruments in the patient's house, which was larger and finer than most peasants' huts, the skin of my hands froze to the cold metal, after which warning I handled them through a towel to prevent a 'cold-burn'. The patient had been delivered of a dead child and some of the placenta had stuck. The village gamps had been at work with unwashed hands and a teaspoon; these measures proving unavailing the old women had used an S-shaped thick wire lamp-hook, rusty and besmeared with greasy soot. The lacerations produced by its use were dreadful.

The professional situation was a delicate one. If I told the gamps what I thought of their methods and of their choice of implements I should make enemies of them, and as I had to leave the patient in their care it was desirable to obtain their friendly assistance. As for instruments, I doubt if there was such a thing in the whole village as a metal tablespoon whose long handle might have served. The lamp-hook seemed to me inexcusable. However, it must be remembered that when face to face with a crisis, and ignorant of the least thing that will remedy the condition, when fear benumbs the mind and one loses contact with one's experience of past difficulties and the way in which to overcome them, then with nearly all of us a stupefying hate surges up, and the crudest and most violent actions are performed in place of more gentle and skilful ones. I was half-sorry for that huddle of shrivelled old women as they passed the hook from one to another, showing it to me as if they felt caught in an evil confederacy and could only excuse their action by giving it the semblance of a joint undertaking. Perhaps it would have been wiser to use their services but I could not trust their obedience; so they were sent to borrow samovars and prepare boiling water, which they could not very well infect.

The details of the gynaecological operation are immaterial. I had to sterilize the instruments three times because of the crawling infestation of cockroaches which ran over the table and dropped from the ceiling. (Cockroaches live on bugs, by the way, so many peasants prefer them in the house; but I, who grow quickly immune to bug bites, prefer these to the restless, rattling scurrying of cockroaches over face and hands when sleeping in the peasants' huts.) I organized as helpers the girls of between fourteen and eighteen who had been to school, hoping thereby to instil, though it be only by a few hours' example and instruction, something of the need for care, cleanliness, and gentleness of touch in these affairs. The village appeared to have about five or six girls of the right age and educability to choose from; they were all given duties.

Eventually the exhausting business was done, and I asked for food. No! I could not have food, did I not remember it was a fast day? I begged for it, said it was near midnight and I had to drive back to the hospital at once (they shuddered); I implored them to give me hot milk, eggs, and bread, saying that the priest had allowed me to give the indulgence of fast-breaking to patients physically in need of food, and I would make it right with their priest if they would give me some. They were adamant. Then I thought of a ruse. I moved the instruments into the kitchen and said I must pack them up myself. They readily agreed, but realizing I was going to steal some bread moved every eatable from the place first. For my comfort perhaps it would have been better if I had employed those old women round the instruments and the bed rather than in merely boiling water in the outer-world of the kitchen; for it was they who raised objection to my taking food, in the belief, I imagine, that it would go ill with the patient if I did.

After seeing about a dozen other patients in the village ('since you are here, doctor!') the patient's brother this time and I set off on the return journey still supperless.

There are two kinds of snowstorm: there is the fluffy kind we have in England, in which snow-flakes fall gently sloping through the breeze and delight us with their cool moist dabbing, and there is the *burran*. It is not only snow that falls in a burran, but also ice-crystals that have lain and become hardened on the ground are picked up by the wind and hurled through the air. The flying ice lashes the skin so that to the pain of cold there is added the torturing bombardment of these sharp, hard particles.

Within half an hour of our departure a *burran* in full strength was upon us. Swiftly it penetrated layer after layer of those sheepskins and the heat of the body was powerlesss to meet and throw off the onset of cold. Exhausted with the night's work, which besides being medically tricky had been socially difficult, I found myself overpowered with sleep. I seemed to be travelling in a curious luminous blue haze; it was cold, of course, but not unpleasant. Sensation was becoming numbed, indeed for some reason being a tiny island in an ocean of cold was not a bad experience. I began to feel an interest in sensations again, the blue haze was rather fascinating and there were faint lights floating or revolving before my sightless gaze. It was quite pleasant to watch their movement which one felt might go on for ever and for ever. Suddenly the faint lights raced in circles and exploded, and at the same time I heard a crash in my skull. I came to with the sledge on top of me in a snowdrift. I had fallen asleep, and so, I imagine, had the driver. In the upset a shaft had been broken.

It is a weary task to mend a sledge shaft by day in still air, there are never any tools but an axe and always too little rope; but in a *burran* at night it is torture. The ropes are stiff with frost, the fingers get so cold that they will not bend to grip the shaft pole, still less the thin hemp cords, and every movement of the limbs is hampered by the mattress-thick layer of sheepskins that one dare not throw off lest the low temperature congeal the muscles into immobility. However, the shaft was mended at last, the horse put back, and on we went; but soon we overturned again. The splice had worked loose, so that the pull of the sledge on the animal becoming suddenly lopsided, he had been thrown one way and we another. Again the struggle with the shafts and cords, and again the horse was put back into harness; but now its nerve had gone and it would not move. So by turns we walked at its head, tapping the snow with the butt of the whip to feel if it were solid under foot, patted the animal's nose, talked to it, and led it along yard by yard. Thus we progressed for, I judge, about an hour. At last the horse took to trotting without being led, so we both got into the sledge and once again dozed off, to be woken up by the stopping of the sledge. We had slid gently into a drift. The driver, having now given up hope, fell on his knees praying, and asked me to join him; 'We will pray and then die'. At this craven and fatalistic suggestion I flew into a rage and knocked him down, asking how he dared to talk about dying, and besides we were pledged to be back in the hospital at eight o'clock in the morning! Then I dumped him in the sledge and tried to stir up the horse. The poor creature was immovable; and although it would obey its master better than it would me I could not trust the peasant on the snow lest he started kneeling again, so I had to lead the horse myself using both the coaxing language and some of those half-Oriental curses which keep Russian horses on the move. By one or other persuasion the animal finally started to trot, so I got back into the sledge for a rest.

But the driver now seemed to have lost his reason. He kept on repeating 'It is foolishness to go on; better die, better die!' Every time he yielded himself to the thought of death my anger was roused afresh; each appeal to resignation was responded to with curses and blows. Under this treatment his view changed; I ceased to be human; it was obvious, he told the Deity, that I was a devil under the protection of Satan. The villagers had rightly called me 'The Great White Devil' (a name I had regarded as an endearment and had ascribed to my large outer coat); it was obvious, he went on in a sort of mixed prayer and conversation with God, why the church bells were never rung for me to guide me when I was out in a snowstorm, the reason why I was thought to be indestructible was now clear—the devil looks after his own. Alternately praying to God and cursing the fiend in the sledge behind him he jogged the horse along.

When he was silent I feared that he had resigned himself once more, so I stirred him up with kicks and oaths, knowing from my experience of anger at him how warming it was! Hour after hour passed in the cursing and fighting of two half-frozen mortals moving painfully over a vast empty expanse of snow under a canopy of hurricane and ice.

At length we saw stacks and hurdles and other outposts of human habitation. It was a khan on the track of a Tartar trade route. So far from our proper and ordinary road were we that I had not even known of the existence of the place. In the starlight we stumbled over sledge ropes and bumped into squatting camels in the courtyard of the khan. It was good to hear their contemptuous guttural grunts (though Russians usually loathe them). We burst into the great kitchen, hot as an oven, where a score of Tartars and Kirkhiz were snoring in their shirts. We took off our sheepskins, held the inner ones against the walls of the oven to warm them, and then, putting them on hot, lay on the floor for an hour's sleep.

The last few miles to the hospital were the worst. After a certain point has been passed the experience of freezing is not painful; the reverse process is an agony of mind and body. The hour's baking in the khan had been the turning-point, so that now, though dawn was breaking and the world was beginning to reshape itself as some external thing that would have to be dealt with, I felt that the task was insupportable through lack of inner strength, and that the pain would go on and on and the spirit sink down and down to an unstruggling and inevitable eternity of suffering. Eventually we arrived at the hospital compound; when passing under the gable end of my house I saw a Siberian crow, which had wintered under the eaves and which I had always looked for with pleasure every morning, frozen dead on the ground. I suppose that the 87° F. of frost registered that night had been more than it could endure. The sight of its stiff body was a shock, but I thought 'I am glad of it! If I know that it is dead I know that I am alive!' In some way that ruthless life-greedy thought produced a change in my mind.

The servants on our arrival were not sure whether it was us or our ghosts; I soon proved which view was correct, for by good fortune a ham had been boiled and was still in the pot, steaming hot. I ate such slabs of it as I thought not possible for a mere human being to consume. But it made no difference; though I knew I was alive my body still felt dead. The hot meat within soon seemed to cool down to the corpse-like temperature of my body; nothing seemed to give the feeling of heat and inner life which sustains our courage and gives a feeling of health though we do not realize this until it is lost. Three times that day the fires were lit in the great stoves and I would have had them relit again but the servants refused lest the overheated stoves burn the house. My table and bed were moved against them, but without effect. For nearly a day my skull felt like a helmet of cold steel under a layer of tepid and scarcely living flesh, the ribs were a chill cuirass which seemed to frost the drawn-in air, the long bones of the arms and legs felt like cold iron bars inserted between the muscles, heavy and chilling from the inside. The horse was laid up for a week and it took the driver two days to recover.

The silly fellow, immediately on our arrival and before taking to his bed, went among his acquaintances in the village and spun them an astonishing tale of the horrors of the night; but it was not the agonizing pain of straining to bend frozen fingers round the shaft and gripping the stiff ropes to lash the broken ends, not the misery of that isolation in the very heart of coldness, no, nor the condition of his sister for whose sake the journey was taken. These were things of this world in which pain is natural. His tale was of having driven a devil who moved under the protection of Satan.

I walked across from my house to the hospital at 8 a.m. to start up work as usual; but this moujik with his yarn had so diverted attention from physical ills to far more interesting metaphysical-theological questions about demons and their like that at first I got nothing from the patients but gaping stares; but soon reluctantly, apologetically even (I am thankful to say not timorously—that nickname was not really taken seriously), they began as usual to tell me of their ailments.

Later I heard that the woman died.

PLACENTA PRAEVIA

A NOTE came one day from a nurse who was working in an outlying village to say that a patient under her care who was before long expecting a child had begun to bleed; the case looked serious and would I come at once.

An examination showed that her urgent summons was justified but that if we took immediate steps the woman could probably be delivered of a living child.

There was the usual crowd of old women in the room observing everything. When not murmuring of comparisons between this terrible event and the score of others they had witnessed, they consoled themselves with short exclamations of piety or with deep sighs which surpassing the physical emptied their souls to the very fundament of woe. These noises are not in themselves disturbing, on the contrary I find in them an echo of my own mood when engaged on obstetric business of unusual difficulty; the worry lay not in their interruptions but in the fact that they might in their ignorance imitate what they thought I had done. In this case all that they would notice was a plunge of the hand nearly to the elbow into the womb, some rummaging about there, then the withdrawal, legs first, of a child. What they would not notice was the careful cleansing of my hands and of the patient and further, what they could not even guess, was why just this particular time is chosen for the work. To their dull eyes and fidgety brains the important thing, the new piece of cunning which they might learn from watching me, would be that dramatic plunge into the interior. It was the master stroke which they would try out when opportunity came, and if they hadn't my magical formula to mumble while doing the trick they would substitute, despite endless failures, one of their own, till they too without harm could thus wrench new life from the bowels of the living.

But these beldames could not be turned away from a spectacle they craved to see, without risk. Among the affairs of men their voices, single or united, amounted to no more than a scranny interruption easily put aside; on matters of childbed, the management of infants, and lastly in the laying out of the dead, these old creatures held absolute sway. All the forces of their lost fertility were turned to a rapacious control of those who in the full heat of youth and maturity held the ardent desires of the present and the growth of the next generation of men in their power. The first question, then, was whether if the crones were turned out of the room they would hold a grudge against the mother and the babe on account of the affront to their position and their pride, saying in later days that an evil spirit had disturbed it in the womb, made the mother gush blood before her time and by another evil spell be delivered. Such a devil-ridden infant is in their view best left to the devil's care if the slightest thing goes wrong with it.

Had I been alone among peasants I should have chosen someone not as helper so much as guardian angel for the child, as guarantor of its true and honourable delivery, but I had with me—a rare event—a fully trained nurse who, of course, for them was a professional rival! To admit the amateur rabble would lower her status, a thing which could not be thought of as she needed as much authority as she could be given. Illness always upsets a home; either there are too few rooms in which the quiet offices of nursing can be performed without interruption or there is no one both suitable and available to watch and wait. Among these peasants there are nearly always helpers in plenty, bunches of them, but they take no individual responsibility, and to get a quiet room is very hard. The huts are small, in them are huddled together six, eight or ten of all ages without privacy of any kind. The personal impact of one person upon another, the desires, loves, hates, love-making, squabbling, clamouring children, discontented whining old age, cause a seething that makes illness doubly trying for the patient. When the occasion demands it the sick nurse must be in a position to requisition a room free from the continual urgency of human associations, she must be in sufficient authority to claim the services of those of her choosing, to inform the relatives (and convey to the patient) that if the house is given up to sick-nursing, the rest finding their lodging elsewhere, it is not because the shadow of death is already darkening the entrance, but that by this seclusion the patient will find a safer and a speedier way to health.

The peasants had primitive ideas about health; there was good health; there was discomfort; and there was illness, this last a dreadful thing bordering on death. A sensible person resisted discomfort for as long as possible, 'went on as usual', until compelled by pain or disturbance of function to call a halt to his labours in the field. Then, and not till then, he lay low, expecting the end at any moment. Only the aged or the maimed allowed it to be seen that they were not capable of a full man's or woman's toil. In convalescence the stages were reversed. A sensible person lay low, brooding within himself and withdrawn until he felt well, then at a turn of time that no one could predict, least of all himself, he would rise and resume his place at the plough or with the axe in the forest. Yesterday he was ill, to-day well: there were no transitions.

Sick-nursing tends to smooth out the stages of recovery, it implies that a person can be ill and yet not nearly dead, can need help of a special kind and yet not be helpless; it introduces the notion of there being different kinds of illness and therefore of special ways of taking care of the body in sickness. Sick-nursing also implies *bodily* disease, and that is a notion which no Russian peasant can grasp; for to them all illness is the evil work of some bad *thing* inside, a foreign body. This alien thing within may be sent from God as a punishment for sins or may be picked up in folly as one gets pricked with brambles if heedless. Illness is an affliction and recovery a blessing—such forces cannot be controlled by man and he should not intervene in the fulfilment of the divine plan.

Such was their view, and this fatalism would have been their practice if another force had not worked on their spirit from within. The love they bore each other made the sight of illness painful and they were glad to get the skilled help of doctors and nurses for those they held beloved and (with inward reservations) for themselves as well. Such help was called only when the condition was past their comprehension, i.e. when the approach of death had been heralded by symptoms that were alarming, or if the patient behaved in an unusual way, as for instance this case of bleeding before labour. They leaned upon doctors for support when in great distress and their minds were ready for the dramatic work of surgery and obstetrics, but nursing in their homes introduced many new complications, it disturbed their ways of thought and needed both a tactful introduction and continual firm support. The chief obstacle, of course, lay in the prejudices of the old women whose emotional life centred on the misadventures of childbirth and the almost voluptuous excitement of laying out the dead. Their power was now twice threatened, first by the passing of their fertile years, and now by the introduction of younger women who neither claimed the affections of men nor brought forth children of their own, but by the exercise of knowledge and by their deft handling of the body in suffering, rose to a position of respect, and more, of affection in the village.

So the old women were coaxed out of the room with the promise that they would be the first to have the news and that they should have a description of what transpired. To make the place quite private, as it had fallen dark, I put clouts over some besoms which I found in an outhouse and propped them against the window panes.

This done I turned to the nurse with some satisfaction and said that with those old biddies out of the way and having the place to ourselves (us two and the patient) it made quite a cosy hospital atmosphere even in a peasant's hut. Nothing irrelevant to intrude, nothing we did would start false ideas going in these greedily curious people—the relief was prodigious.

From my first arrival with the nurse to the exclusion of the old women was perhaps the matter of a quarter of an hour. We now set to work busily; arranged tables, sterilizers, instruments and chloroform all neatly to hand, had lamps hanging in just the right place and everything ready.

The nurse and I worked together swiftly and in silence. The patient needed a whiff of chloroform, which acted I think more by suggestion than by its anaesthetic property, for she needed only a few drops, and its administration by the nurse was skilfully done. The delivery—after that plunge of the arm—was straightforward, and was followed by the afterbirth with very small delay. At this dramatic moment I heard a gentle but long-drawn-out '*k-k-oo-oo*'. 'What are you saying, nurse?' 'Nothing, I didn't speak.' I was puzzled, for I could have sworn someone spoke, and that it wasn't the patient; it was an articulated sound, not the relaxed puffing or stertorous gargling noise of a person under an anaesthetic, and I did not think the mother was then fully under.

It was a finely shaped child, with no moles or other devil's marks upon which malice could fasten, and in a trice she was breathing. The mother was soon round and comfortable. I was sweating with the nervous strain, for it's a touch and go matter at the best of times, and it seemed to me a good day's work. I flung myself on a stool, leaned back against the wall and looked up at the ceiling while I wiped my forehead—and there only five feet above the bed in full view of it was a row of boys' and girls' faces. Half a dozen of them.

When clearing the hut of all but the nurse and the patient I had forgotten to look for the shelf which hangs about two feet from the ceiling and runs about five or six feet out from the wall. It is used for stowage, but often enough the members of the family old enough to climb and young enough to be wanted out of the way house themselves there for the night and lie chattering and wriggling, listening to their elders and watching all that goes on till sleep overtakes them.

I was mightily annoyed, at them without reason and at myself with some cause, for having overlooked the common hiding-place; so I hauled them out and gave them a smack on the bottom apiece, telling them not to watch such doing again, and be off!

The nurse and I had a good laugh when they were gone and then ushered in the old women, but it was no longer possible for them to be the first to have details of the birth. They were not, however, angry at the children having been there, because they were only children, they did not matter, their turn had not yet come for the rub of birth and death.

Then in came the proud grandmother, chewing a rag in which was pocketed bacon rind and baked flour; this she was about to pop into the child's mouth to be the first intruding touch from the outside world when I stopped her, and asked her to consider whether it was as nice and clean a comforter as the mother's breast; and, besides, had she not got pyorrhoea (her gums were awash with pus)—in fact, the usual hygienic pleas. It was an ill-judged if not unkind interruption, because in any case the cosy rag would be thrust in the moment our backs were turned and by giving the babe something she had herself chewed she was in an animal sort of way binding her love to it as best she knew how.

There was no need to be worried over the nurse's status in the villages. The half-dozen young witnesses gave a full version of how she had killed the woman with a rag wet from a bottle while I had gouged the brat out with my arm, and then between us we had pulled both round to life again. With them the exciting spectacle would only give colour to their dreams; they were too young to crave for the details as a means of holding in their jealous grip the destinies of a younger generation.

*   *   *   *   *

An earlier experience had made me nervous of the use these old women would make of medical knowledge. One old woman came to hospital because her belly was becoming distended with fluid. She was admitted and was 'tapped'. The word, I suppose, is borrowed from the brewers; in this case the vast tun of her abdomen was broached with a medium-sized trochar and cannula. The patient was told to look away—for further security and to give her comfort a nurse kept her hand over her eyes; she was told 'It is just a prick', then came a quick jab, the silver tube was plunged up to the hilt, the trochar removed and a rubber tube put over the spouting jet of ascitic fluid—all in a matter of seconds. The rubber tube led over the bedside to a bucket and when the rate of flow had been arranged to be neither too quick nor too slow, and all was covered up, the patient was told to look round now and see how nice everything was! Indeed, she had hardly felt anything, a prick, that was all. The hours passed, and the full buckets were removed, measured and returned empty to the ward; meal-time came; bandages were gradually tightened, to haul in the slack; the orderly routine of a small hospital doing a small operation in an efficient, tidy way, was pleasing to the patient and to ourselves.

When the fluid was out of the way it was possible to make a proper examination; this done, she was told that the fluid would return—secondary growths were numerous—but that its removal would be no more unpleasant than on this occasion. She was to use her discretion, not to put off coming till the discomfort was unsupportable, nor on the other hand to come every few days, but say once a month or so.

In six or seven weeks she returned, staggering under her caskful of fluid. Again she went through the simple procedure. She was put to bed, a nurse came and held her hand over her eyes, another nurse dabbed her belly with something wet (iodine), the doctor jabbed at her (a mere prick), then some fuss with buckets, the bed-clothes rearranged, and finally with a 'there now!' all was over once more and she had an afternoon in a little whitewashed room, occupied besides herself by two or three other women. All settled down for a good chat.

A third time she came, at a rather shorter interval, and she was by now quite at home with us, full of praises for our help to her, and how great was our cleverness.

On the fourth visit she was more thoughtful. She asked to be allowed to watch the procedure; we told her that it would be exactly the same as before so she need not worry. Her head was averted, the procedure in all details carried out quite smoothly, but she was still worried. After a time, she said, 'You see, doctor, I do want to know just what you do to me.' She was told that nothing more was done but to drain the fluid away. 'Yes,' she replied, 'I understand that, but what I can't get hold of is the method you use. Will you show me the thing you do it with?' It is not a doctor's habit to do such a thing; but, overcome by her persuasions, another trochar and cannula was fetched similar to the one that was then in use but a size smaller, not that there was much in that. She handled it with great respect and began to give the reason for her curiosity.

She had been an object of interest in her village, leaving it in the morning so big and so inert, returning in the evening so slim and full of life. At the vapour baths she was an object of comment, and the other women there began with a spread of hands to ask if she could last out another week, and so forth.

On one occasion during this banter their sharp eyes spied a girl also growing big in the belly, and contrasting her with my patient they said that she was filling up in another way—and what wonder, a fine healthy wench ... and who was the father ... she had kept it pretty quiet—and so on, bathroom gossip. But the girl took it otherwise, swore to them that she had no relations with a man, it was no baby at all; to which they replied, 'We will wait and see!'

The patient turned the matter over in her mind and, after another bout of this teasing, approached the girl with an offer. She was by now an expert in this fluid business, and if it was as the girl said no baby at all, then from her experience she knew the remedy.

Next week at the baths the matter came up again. Again the girl denied before the company of women any connexion with a man; again the patient said that if it were so, then it must be fluid, and she knew how to drain it off. She had brought with her a kitchen knife. At the sight of it the girl's resolution almost broke, but, being reminded of her denials of pregnancy, she yielded to the view that it must be fluid. At this she was urged by the old woman to have it drained away. With the words 'It is just a prick', she drove the kitchen knife into the girl's belly below the navel, 'and doctor, she lay three days dying'.

There was a pause after she had said this. She turned the silver cannula and the fine-pointed steel trocher over and over in her hands, and added as if a doubt had now been cleared up, 'I thought you used a knife!'

There was only one question after that to put to her: 'Why, if you thought it fluid, did you not send her to the hospital?' She made no reply and gave no sign that she thought the question contained a good or bad idea. The situation was baffling; one was not sure whether this was ignorance more profound than one had dreamed possible or malice so infiltrated into the character that it left no stirring of remorse even after a killing—she could not accommodate herself to her guilt.

THE APOLOGY

SOME TIME before the Bolsheviks were even heard of in our part of Russia, I was driving at dusk through a village on my way back to hospital when a drunken peasant jumped on to the runners of the sledge and demanded that I should stop and treat his headache. He tried to drag me from the sledge by force, so I put my foot on the pit of his stomach and pushed him into a snowdrift. His manner and the strong language he used when he rose were such that a more exact diagnosis and a more medical treatment of his condition did not seem to be indicated. My driver, remarking that the fellow would have a worse head next morning, whipped up the horses and drove on. The trivial incident passed out of my mind.

One day, months later when the snow had gone, an unusual thing happened. A peasant in the waiting-room of the out-patients asked to be seen *last*, in contrast to the usual clamour to be seen first. When all the other comers had been attended to, the moujik, standing rather shyly by the door, said 'Doctor, don't you recognize me?' I looked at him carefully and said I did not, then turning to the out-patient register, asked when he had been before and what his trouble was. He said he had never been before and had no ailment, but before proceeding he must know that I recognized him. I told him to come to the point; if he had not been before and was not ill what knowledge had I of him, and what did he want of me in the hospital now? 'Doctor, if I tell you, you won't be angry with me, will you?' I searched my mind for possible wrongs received, things stolen from the hospital or my house, swindlings at the fortnightly fair where I had bought sheep and pigs; but remembered nothing amiss that I could associate him with and gave him my word I would not be angry.

'Do you remember months ago in the village of —— a drunken man set upon you as you were driving through and demanded that you should stop?' The scene came back in a flash. 'And do you remember,' I said, smiling, 'the doctor who put his foot in that man's belly and gave a shove? Damn it all, man; we were quits.'

'Now doctor, don't make a joke of it. It's a serious matter.' I thought I must have injured him, so apologized and asked him to tell me all about it.

He then began a long story. He had been drunk and felt sick and thick in the head; so seeing me, he suddenly had the bright idea of demanding an instant cure. But his headache made him angry and he tried to do this by force. He had attacked me and that was wrong. Before he asked my forgiveness, it was necessary that I should know exactly who he was and recall the circumstances. He then very shyly produced a document which ran roughly as follows:

This is to certify that I [here there was a space for my name] have received the apology of —— ——, of the village of ——, on the [space for the date]. And this is also to certify that the elders of the said village of ——, after careful examination are convinced that ——— ———'s apologies are from the heart. [Date, signatures of village elders and crosses of attestation.]

The whole thing seemed fantastic; an apology was in the circumstances odd but understandable, but the certificate seemed all out of proportion. I made up my mind to see the village elders and try to clear the matter up.

A few days later my round lay through that village and I called on several of the elders. They said they had been horrified by the attack on me. I had done them no harm, on the contrary had been diligent for their good, and it was necessary to eradicate the evil disposition which had shown itself amongst them that night. I pointed out that my quite adequate physical defence had prevented injury to me being laid on the man's conscience, and also that I had attended patients in the village after the episode just as before, so they need not fear the loss of my assistance; but that was not the point. They felt the attack to be a stain on the honour of the village. They had reproached him next day and asked him to apologize. He was defiant in refusal (perhaps through the humiliation of having been rolled over in the snow) and finally brought forward in extenuation the obvious fact that he had been intoxicated. But this for them was no excuse; when sober one must make amends for one's deed when drunk. Then, since as a group they had not been able to persuade him to apologize, they changed their policy and approached him as individuals. They also got his friends to join in their efforts and for weeks the poor devil was followed wherever he went with reproachful eyes. One day he burst upon them with the news that he would go and apologize. But his manner of saying it did not satisfy them; it was hasty and still somewhat defiant; his heart had not changed. They accepted his consent to apologize as a good sign but not necessarily as an indication of true repentance. Gradually he became more passive and waited patiently to be 'released' by the village elders from the yoke of guilt. He then came to me with their certificate.

This narration left several things unexplained. This repentant sinner had been brought once more within their most sensitive and intimate circle, he had become again what the village calls 'one of us'; after months of communion with him he had been found to be pure in heart. Why then did they need my signature to the certificate of release? Did it mean, I asked, that they could not after all trust him to apologize? They said that they did not distrust him, but that they wished me to know that they felt themselves also to be involved in the insult and hence also in the restoration of the honour of the village.

This was their explanation. There were, of course, other reasons for dealing with me in this way. A physician was an object of value to them. They were helplessly dependent on him and his goodwill, and however familiar he might be as a visitor in their homes and at their councils, they *as a group* could not replace or reproduce him because he belonged to a different civilization, that of the metropolis and of international communications. Towards all members of this civilization they looked with abject submission, envy, and sometimes hatred; from the metropolitan civilization came to them tax gatherers, political police (civil order was maintained, as this story shows, by the villagers themselves in a most unbureaucratic way), landlords (for the most part absentee), priests, a few schoolteachers, and a very few doctors. These, one and all, belonged to the metropolis, not to the village. Over all loomed the distant and terrible, revered and incomprehensible figure of the Czar, who, however widely his characteristics ranged over everything Russian, certainly was not 'one of us'.

It was a sign of affection and trust in me that the village elders did not themselves come crawling to me with an apology, but a sign of latent fear that made them send the certificate. A not unfriendly representative of an alien world, I belonged to the town, distant from them though familiar with their village ways. The gulf between us narrowed when the relationship was personal, widened when it touched on the doctor's position in the social structure.

This little episode shows something of the way in which the villagers were bound together by ties of love and how they kept the spirit of their community intact. This spirit gave the members strength when they were in accord with it, and they lived in misery and isolation when they broke, in thought or mood, with the opinion and sentiment of their neighbours. The episode also shows how difficult it was for them to include a member of the alien caste in their way of thought and living.

* * * * *

Some of the social history of the next few years is well known. The Bolsheviks came to power and made all things new. The peasants were collectivized, many were forcibly moved to public works, many more were driven by starvation to seek a living in the towns. The new social unit became the factory, and the old village organization ceased to be typical for the Russian people. But its spirit did not die.

Seventeen years passed, and an Intourist traveller brought back from one of the large new cities a collection of factory wall-newspapers (the placards on which anyone may freely criticize anyone and anything except the essentials of the new régime). Most of the contents related to the factory statistics, how the shock workers were breaking records, sport, the factory theatre, music news, and so forth. Down in a corner (always the same corner of each issue) there was a series of notes which at first glance seemed of the most trivial significance. But their spirit was reminiscent of the village I have mentioned, and heaven knows how many thousand like it. The notes ran somewhat as follows: 'We do not like the way Sonia ——— does her work. She doesn't show the right spirit; she slacks.' Several times was she thus publicly reproved. Later she was said to show signs of adopting the proper attitude. Finally Sonia was declared an enthusiastic worker who had entered truly into the spirit of the Revolution.

On reading this my mind went back to the peasant whose heart was changed by the silent but not harsh pressure of the group; the steps in this re-entry into the community seemed to be remarkably similar in the two cases; in spite of the greatest imaginable change in the economic and political life the behaviour of the group to a wayward member remained the same. The village spirit, the need to feel that everyone was 'one of us', had re-emerged; and I have no doubt that this plays its part in strengthening and consolidating a régime which often seems to us in the West to be based only on force.

THE THREAT

CLINICAL WORK is much the same the world over because the response to physical disease is little affected by race or climate; but the doctor's work is greatly affected by the social conditions, the administrative complexity (or over-simplicity), and even the climate in the area of his labours. Sometimes difficulties arise from issues quite outside the proper limits of medical activity.

When I was acting as a county council doctor in Russia I had to cover single-handed an area about the size of Surrey and a population of at least 50,000 of half a dozen different races. The problem was to distribute the small amount of medical aid where it would be most effective and was most needed, irrespective of other considerations. A few outlying clinics were established (at about twenty miles from the central hospital) which I visited on weekly rounds so as to save patients the burden of travel; they were placed after careful consideration of the population and general healthiness of the neighbourhood. To prevent unnecessary delays I stopped at villages *en route* to these clinics only if I had previous notice of illness that must be seen at home, or if more than a handful of out-patient cases was reported.

One route passed through a small village of independent colonists from Little Russia, people of vigorous disposition and, as it happened, good bodily health. The headman of the village, who had seen me drive through several times, requested me to place a clinic in his village, but this was declined on the ground that his village was small, quite near another clinic, and, above all, remarkably healthy. He offered to provide a room free: 'And would you', I asked, 'let me see all comers there?'

'We certainly would not, it would of course be for our own people!' It would be a disgrace, he added, for his villagers to mix themselves with the ordinary peasants among my out-patients; his people were above such mud and desired special consideration. He admitted that one of his chief reasons for wanting the clinic was prestige, as he had promised his villagers that he would obtain it. I refused on the ground of medical urgency elsewhere.

The next time I drove through on my round I noticed an unusual number of dogs barking, and realized that they were being set on us. The horses, though frightened, kept up a good pace. One of the wolf-like beasts nearly got on to the sledge, but having to run after us it did not quite manage the final leap. Shortly after a note came from the headman. Would the clinic be opened? Again it was refused. I resolved next time to go through his territory prepared. A week later my driver asked if I would not make my round by another way; but this I would not do, and we set out.

There are few things pleasanter than a sledge drive across the Steppe on a sunny morning. There is a sting in the air, the snow under the runners squeaks crisply, and the muffled thumping of the horses' feet and the rocking of the sledge over the undulating ground produce a peaceful contentment. The best kind of sledge is one with a level floor big enough to hold a truss of hay, which, skilfully spread out and covered with sheep-skins, is more comfortable than any contrivance of seats and springs. By jamming one's feet in one corner, sprawling diagonally across the sloping mound of hay, and bracing one's shoulders into the opposite corner of the back one can by a quick stiffening of the body grip the sledge, as it were, when it crashes into a deep bump or heels over on an incline, and one's arms are free to be tucked into the long sleeves of the sheepskin outer overcoat. The shaft-horse is attached only at the collar, the shafts being kept very wide apart by the great arch of wood on which the bells are hung. The traces of the leading horse are long enough to leave eight or ten feet between the leader's tail and the shaft-horse's nose, so that the leader can swerve round bumps and potholes and pull the forward end of the shafts into the right direction. This also permits the leader to pick a good surface by allowing him a wide lateral range of move-ment. But the leader must have good nerves, for if he runs wild the sledge will crash, the shafts be broken, and the curved-up front of the runners may break the shaft-horse's legs. The distance between the horses necessi-tates two whips, one with a thong about six feet long for the near animal, and one about thirty feet long for the trace-horse. These whips dangle from the driver's wrists, and their long thin strands of twisted leather ride over the snow with an arching and rippling movement like attendant serpents keeping pace on either side of the sledge.

On this morning our horses slowed down at a hill and rested at the top. Below us lay the village we must pass through. The wall and fence that surrounded it were banked up with snow into sloping ramparts, cut by the road that passed through the middle of the village, which was guarded by a gate at either end. It was a quiet scene and I noticed that both gates were open. The driver started the horses and we raced down the hill at a full gallop. He went through the first gate superbly, and we were doing the quarter-mile of village street at a speed and in a style that Russians love. When we had gone part way through the village they let the dogs loose. This time the dogs bore down upon us from the front so that they had the advantage of a springing attack. They worried the horses, which slowed down enough to make it possible for the brutes to jump full on me and to get over the back of the low-built sledge. I had already disconnected the two portions of a cranioclast and held them in readiness. I got up and, standing by the driver, dealt with those that came upon us from the sides, while he with the whips tried to keep them clear of the horses. Then, to my surprise, the villagers, who had stood and watched the scene, whistled to their dogs; this caused a momentary distraction which allowed the horses to spring into a gallop.

But the villagers had not done with us yet. There was the second gate to shoot through, and some of them standing nearby released more dogs at us from the flank in order to head the trace-horse up the rise of snow that had banked up to the level of the top of the wall, where an overturn would have been inevitable, and a ghastly mauling by dogs a certainty as we floundered to our feet. The horses were in panic, the sledge was swerving from side to side of the road, but by masterly driving they were kept off that dreadful slope, and we made a clean exit through the open gate.

The rest of the day was uneventful.

Some weeks later I was called from supper. Would I go at once to a desperately ill woman? A fast sledge had been sent for me and the village was only twelve miles away. Without thought or discussion I stepped into the sledge, and was driven off at a fine spanking pace. I soon saw that the route lay towards that village. Then I noticed little details: the carriage of the driver's head, the cut of his coat, the shape of the sledge—all seemed familiar and yet made a pattern that was different from the usual one in my neighbourhood, and I realized suddenly that I was going not through but *to* that village.

We drew up at the headman's house and I was led straight to his mother who was certainly very ill with pneumonia. I did what could be done about diet, explained about nursing, and then wrote a prescription to be made up at my hospital. As soon as that was done the headman said, 'And now about that clinic!' I told him the answer was the same, and further that to set dogs on doctors was not the way to get a clinic. 'Very well,' he said, 'if you don't consent you can get home by yourself, my horses shall not take you and I am not going to be responsible for what the dogs do to you.' To his shame this was said in his mother's hearing. I saw only one way out of the difficulty, apart from agreeing to set up a clinic where he wanted it and not where it was needed.

Acting instantly on the knowledge that a prescription is regarded by these people with superstitious reverence, I replied, 'The burden of that decision falls on other shoulders' and tore the prescription to pieces. To *my* shame this also was said and done in the patient's presence. He took the dreadful blow to his mother with steadiness and said quietly that I had beaten him. I immediately promised to send the medicine at once on my return to the hospital if he would have me driven back and no more dogs were set on me. I said I would visit serious cases in his village as I was doing at that moment and would stop on my way through if requested in the customary way; but no clinic, and no more dogs. He kept his bargain and I mine. I do not know what happened to his prestige.

These hardy independent people were a fine set of men, if somewhat rough. It is a misfortune for which individuals are not to blame that when an aggressive attitude towards life finds outlet in communal action the leaders of the group are often rich in cunning, though poor in wisdom. The people I have described had different, but equally admirable, qualities from the more numerous, more lazy, more gregarious village-peasants of Great Russia; unfortunately the two types did not get on well together. The world now knows such sturdy independent farmers in the heart of Soviet Russia by the name of *Kulaks*. And I for one, who saw something of their mettle, regret, though can understand some of the reasons for, their liquidation.

THE BRIDAL DRESS

One of my recurrent duties when on my rounds in a nearby village was to visit and watch the progress or the deterioration, as the turns of her illness took her, of an eighteen-year-old girl who had tuberculosis. She was of an amiable disposition and, knowing what ailed her and what was probably in store, met the changes of her condition with resignation. Before one of my holidays she was worse and I did not think it likely that I would see her again.

On my return I went to that village a day or so earlier than I expected, for I was called out late in the evening to another case. Being so near I thought I would look up the girl; I told the driver to wait while I went on foot, the better to enjoy the freshness of the summer night. From a distance I heard the hollow wooden sounds of carpentry, and the little house where the girl lay was lit up. The lamplight fell on the low whitewashed fence surrounding the little garden and the boughs of a silver birch dipped into the shafts of light and lifted again into the darkness as the wind swayed the trees. Within doors the scene was also one of brightness and animation. From a distance I could see people in festival dress moving about under the lamps, so many lamps that they must have been borrowed for the gay occasion. She must have turned the corner, I thought; quickening my steps I came to the little fence by the garden and saw her sitting up in bed, far prettier than of late, her hair in plaits hung down neatly, her cheeks looked plump, her posture, so different from the sunken invalid I had left, was trim and alert. She sat very still and her eyelids looked heavy—fatigue, I first thought: but she was dead.

The sounds of carpentry followed me down the village street as, not wishing to join in the wake nor share the labour of her brothers making her coffin, I returned to the waiting horses.

She lay in the dress she would have worn as a bride, and which if worn as a bride she would have treasured, kept tidy and neatly folded till its second bridal appearance, when she would enter the Kingdom of Heaven once more a girl, fresh in the glory of her youth, rejoicing in her Lord.

'Tell me, doctor,' I have often been asked by some old women as I have stood by their bedsides, 'how soon will it be that I wear my bridal dress?—this autumn, maybe; the spring perhaps?'—wheedling out of me if possible a date that they can look forward to. It will be *their* day once more; their hair will be done in plaits, their hands crossed over the blessed sign of Jesus, they will be carried aloft over the heads of men, to lie on the top of the hill for ever and ever in the holy company of angels.

POLICE

Soon after my appointment as Resident at a county hospital in the district of Buzuluk in the government of Samara, I was honoured by a visit from the chief of police of the neighbourhood. He was very polite, and offered to assist me so far as he was able. If I got into trouble with the peasants, I had merely to call on the constables, and everything would be put right. I was told that the police had genuine Tashkent horses worth six hundred roubles, and if I cared for riding he was sure everything could be arranged. Finally he mentioned that his daughter was dying of heart disease and would I see her.

During the frequent visits that that disease involved, I became acquainted with the family, and found the report true that the chief of police was as kind-hearted as any man in the province. The peasants respected him and no one had a bad word for him. His usual price was three roubles, but any work which he did for the people involving extensive silence called for a higher rate. People said that they respected the way in which he took money—he was friendly, easy, and gave confidence without 'stooping to the people' or lowering himself in any way.

One day the village postman burst into the out-patients' department with a notice. He said, with a meaning smile, that he hadn't time to discuss it then, but there would be plenty of time later. It was the last official manifesto from Nicholas the Second—his abdication. With it was a circular which began, 'At last. It has happened!' and went on to encourage the people by telling them that liberty lay in their hands, and that, if they used self-restraint, they would enjoy the privileges they had so long coveted.

I nailed the notice up on the wall, and proceeded with my work. The peasants came into the consulting-room beaming with delight. 'Well, so he's gone, just think of that: and he has been our Czar for God knows how many years, and when he leaves us everything will be the same as ever. I suppose he will go to manage his estates somewhere; he always liked farming'—and so on. Only an old woman cried, 'Poor man! he never did anyone any harm; why did they put him away?'

She was interrupted: 'Shut thy mouth, thou old fool! They aren't going to kill him; he's run away, that's all.'

'Oh, but he was our Czar, and now we have *no one*!'

In the village street I met the chief of police; he forced a grim smile and said, 'Now I'm unemployed. Look at this.' And he slapped his left hip, 'Unarmed! And I, chief of police, this morning gave up my sword to a woman! In *Russia*!'

He turned, and we walked down the street to the square; but he would not go into the village council-room, as he still felt a little bit ridiculous in the presence of that fat woman. The person in question was a school-teacher from a neighbouring village who, because of her executive ability and public service in the past, had been chosen to fill the post of Keeper of Public Order for the time being.

Several weeks passed without anything of note happening, till the time drew near for a local horse-fair which attracted thousands of people from outlying districts. In the old régime, this had always been a time of anxiety for the police, so we were anxious to see how the schoolmistress would cope with the situation. Going out to the fair, I noticed twelve old men, greybeards, walking with long staves very like a Greek chorus, each wearing an armlet of white linen. I went up to one and asked him who they were.

He said, 'We are the militia. It is my first day out and I feel a bit foolish, but it will be all right in an hour or two when I get to talking with some of the people.'

I asked what his duties were.

'God knows. I'll just do what they all do.'

This militia was in force for several months. One or two old men, when appointed by their village councils to the duty, wrote to me asking for medical certificates that they were too old and feeble. The matter became so pressing that I paid a special visit to one village council to inquire what I had better do. The elders said that my sole criterion was to be real physical disease; they told me that they specially selected old men because they had tact and judgement and were of all people least likely to antagonize a young man if he was drunk and disorderly; they said that no one would dream of knocking down an old greybeard, whereas, if they appointed a young man as militiaman, there would be trouble all the time. 'We don't need to be kept in order, we only need to be re-minded.'

The deserting soldiers contributed with several other causes to produce a new militia. In my district I was told so many times that I should be shot if I did not give certificates of exemption from army service, that I wrote to headquarters requesting that a military tribunal should settle the cases in the villages. The threatenings among Russian villagers are as a rule much more serious than the shootings. After a few weeks such a tribunal was instituted, and a military militia came into the district. In the middle of the summer several men in our village took exception to me because I was a friend of the ex-policeman, and must therefore be a counter-revolutionary. I received 'warnings', and anonymous notes telling me of my danger were slipped under my door in the early hours of the morning (one written by the daughter of my would-be murderer).

Of course, nothing happened. The friends of my critic told the military militia of the danger I was in, in order to get the militia to take sides and so divide the village sentiments. But the militia said that it was 'all nonsense', and that the whole affair would blow over. About a week later the would-be murderer was admitted to the hospital for scalp wounds because he had told the villagers that they were not revolutionary enough. Perhaps he was the first Bolshevik we had in our village. Everyone was sorry for him—they said he was a bit 'cracked'.

The militia went away in the fall, and the village elected constables of their own. Not old men this time, but middle-aged men who were serving on the council. On one occasion it was discovered that four men whom the village trusted had been robbing the village coffers. An enraged people, on hearing their confession, led them out into the public square and clubbed them to death. Next day they were buried at the public expense, and their families pensioned.

Under the latter days of the Bolsheviks, a few of the Red Army were put in charge of the villages—poor frightened boys armed and set against the trained fighters of the allied Czechs and Cossacks. When the writer left, the village was patrolled by Cossacks, and the villagers lived in terror. I asked the people why they were frightened and they said, 'Because they are Cossacks and we know them'.

When working for order in Russia there are two opposing agents between which we must choose:[1] the force of the police and Cossacks, and the influence of the village elders. A peasant said to me, explaining the police, 'When a Russian is armed by the government he is made into a brute. We do not use force in our villages because it stands between men; our way brings them together.' And judging from my own experience, the period when greybeards were clothed in authority was the period of greatest security and of fullest development of political and domestic life.

[1] Written in 1919.

PEASANT OFFICERS

ONE DAY after seeing a great number in the out-patient department, close on a hundred, I was poring over my notes with some attention and did not notice that I was no longer alone, for on chancing to raise my eyes I saw there before me not a villager but an apparition. The dull log walls of the out-patient room were lit by the presence of a handsome young Caucasian officer in full and shining uniform. When I looked up he clicked heels and saluted. I shook hands and waved him to a seat, asking what on earth brought him to visit me; for there was not a look of worry held firmly in the background which darkens the faces at consultation of the young and otherwise healthy when they come with venereal disease. He seemed at peace with himself and the world. His movements were swift, strong, and graceful, without a trace of the lumbering movement of the peasant. Their action seems as from habit to wait upon the common will, the motion of each limb follows the slow deliberation of a hesitating soul, whereas the gestures of the fine young animal before me were the muscular expression of a single independent mind. 'I was waiting till you had finished', he said, 'my business is not urgent. Two of my brothers are back from the front and we are all rather worried about my father's health; so I came to ask if you would look him over; he says there's nothing to bother about, but we don't like the look of things at all.'

This was altogether puzzling; first of all an officer who does not swagger or get impatient was in itself a rare event; then his voice, strong and quiet, was one I could not place, it had none of the clipped city-bred culture, nor the peasants' drawl; finally I wondered where his father could at this moment be lying. I knew most of the landowners round about but he did not resemble them.

I got my case of instruments and went with him. A rather shabby carriage was at the door; we got in and, without a word to or from the driver, were off. He pulled up at a peasant's house, bigger than most, without a trace of luxury, but there was a shelf of books—an unusual thing. It had a single large room capable of being warmed in winter, and a cold outhouse in which lived the usual collection of chickens and calves.

In the room there were already nine adults; our three selves made twelve. Three of those I judged to be sons were in officers' uniform, a fourth in the ranks, all as clean, neat, well shaved, with trim hair-cut, polished boots, and as well-ordered, brushed tunics as you could find in all Russia. A peasant of about sixty-five lay on a bed, his wife and a girl of about twenty were busy by the stove, a young woman had a baby at the breast, and another rather more slatternly-looking stood about doing nothing. A peasant boy sat at a table finishing a meal and there was besides myself also the driver. Only one looked ill, the peasant on the bed, so I went over to him and after a greeting said, referring to the Caucasian officer, 'Is this your son?' He laughed and said, 'You look surprised. Yes, he is my son all right and these are his brothers.' I was introduced to the officers and the private, and with equal pride to the peasant chewing at the table and to the driver. He had daughters which he indicated in a general way.

Four of his six boys had gone to seek their fortunes in the towns. The war came and they had been drafted into the army; the pre-revolutionary chaos came, and by their ability they had risen to officers' rank, in two cases with transfer of regiment, hence the Caucasian accoutrements; the revolution came, and they had gone back to their village to see how things were faring there. This done they would go back to the army, and when the fighting was over they would return to the life of the city again, unless their help was needed in the village. Two of the officers were likely to settle down in city life, one was married to a town girl, another engaged, the ranker didn't know what he would do, the officer who came for me would continue in the army if there seemed likelihood of proper work, if not he was as content to follow the plough.

The father began by telling me of his sons, and of how popular they were in the village; but of none was he so proud as of the two who were farmers because they seemed the best natured; this was spoken, of course, aloud, and in the hearing of the other four. My discomfort at hearing these gentle family discriminations in Russia was slowly vanishing, because they appeared to be signs of solidarity and unity in the family, rather than occasions of bitterness.

I asked why he was not proud of his officer sons. He said the country could be proud of them, because their worth was shown in the country's wars; but his home-staying sons had shown their worth in the village and home; therefore he was proudest of them because he was a plain villager himself.

The old peasant was more communicative about them after his 'army boys' left. Their career and abilities were a source of pride, but he was more gratified by the fact that success had in no way altered their friendliness to their stay-at-home brothers, nor their interest (not mere curiosity) in the village. 'They can go away and they can come back; that is a great thing.'

It is indeed a great thing to be able to acquire the independence which city life brings, the capacity for quick decisions, to feel the emergence into consciousness of personal ambition, and then to shed these new-found instruments of satisfaction, to yield them up and lean with an utter reliance on the public will, becoming once more with perfect resignation 'one of us'.

Those who get bitten by the pushing egoistic life of the towns usually return at longer intervals to their villages, till finally they form part of that uprooted proletariat without a village (communal) life or an urban (mob) life, which though gutter-streaked and apparently degraded has sometimes a tradition and at all times an immense reserve of strength. Until they have found themselves again in politics or in an organized occupation these cultural no-man's-landers are the loneliest souls on earth.

I think the extent—and, indeed, the pain—of this

cultural rootlessness may have contributed a good deal to the revolution. The brutality, not merely the bloodshed, of the revolutionaries could only have come about —at least, as far as I understand Russians—in the presence of much isolation in the minds of very many men from the corporate spirit of their fellows. The economic factor, about which much has been said, is there as well of course, but I have missed from the writings and the lecturings I have heard on the Russian Revolution a sufficient understanding of the part played by the interaction of two forces—the strength of personal ambition and the 'pull' of another force leading to submission to the group. The former is found in an almost pure form in the old régime bureaucracy, the latter, again in almost pure form, in the peasantry. (These two forces do not mix readily together; the task of the new régime,[1] to make a modern state out of Old and Holy Russia, was and is far greater than Western observers commonly realize.)

In the old régime there were two societies facing one another, the Bureaucracy and the Peasants, the Rulers and the Ruled. No position between these two was satisfactory, no Russian, to use the language of another culture, could really believe that it pleased God to call him to any other station but those of the extremes; there was no middle-class content; nor could there be when those of the middle looked above and below them with mingled yearning and moral or physical repulsion.

[1] Written in 1919.

A POLITICAL EPISODE

THE POLITICAL events in Petrograd following the abdication of the Czar and the setting up of the Provisional Government were much discussed in our village, but they did not affect our lives to any great extent.

One day a deputation came to me from the village; its members were shy about making their request but would I kindly stand as their candidate for the Constituent Assembly shortly to be summoned in Petrograd. The request filled me with an almost overwhelming sense of littleness and humility, and of compassion for the good folk who were driven to such an extremity. It was an endearing request and though the thought of being mixed up in city politics was most distasteful, that fact had to be concealed from the villagers out of consideration for their feelings. Then I thought of a way out: 'But I am an Englishman!' 'So was Tom Paine,' said a tousled-headed old moujik, 'but he sat in the Constituent Assembly in Paris'; several gave assent to this.

Interest in the distant events in the capital, however important they might be for the future of Russia, receded from my mind; a fact of major importance demanded immediate attention. How came this illiterate old man, shielded for generations from every political influence by an enormous force of political police, to know of Tom Paine? I knew the moujik and his villagers well, or thought I did, was invited to their weddings, baptisms, and funerals, and to the meetings of the *mir*, had often talked into the night on every sort of subject including politics (though of the latter much more after the abdication than before), but I never guessed such *knowledge* existed among them. They had questioned me at length about the political system in England, and I had explained about our two-party system of Liberals and Conservatives, and of how sometimes the Conservatives passed measures which had been prepared and begun under the Liberals, and the other way round too. (On hearing this, which astonished them, one old gaffer said 'I'll go and tell that to my horse; if he understands I too will believe that there may be some sense in it'.) Of curiosity there was no limit and each point was discussed among them with thoroughness and a good deal of common sense; but the *knowledge* was another matter, of that they showed nothing until that remark about Tom Paine.

About forty years before this time an educated man had gone from village to village putting up in the peasant houses and telling them in the evenings of the liberation of the people in various countries and of the French Revolution in particular; he was probably a Narodnik. My informant had heard of this as a boy and had told his children: thus was history taught and passed on. Had the abdication occurred a half-century later and another Englishman had made a similar excuse in declining the invitation I have little doubt he would have received the same answer but from this old fellow's grandson.

From long habits of caution, the caution natural to peasants reinforced by the fear of the police, there was never a parade of knowledge, before me at least, of any facts that were not within the common experience of every member of the *mir*. But after this revelation I saw that the instances they adduced from their village experience were sometimes selected with respect to, but without reference to, other events of which they had knowledge. The peasants talked much and they gossiped freely, so that one got to know who was pregnant by whom, and where and when, and who had an abortion and whether it was to be hushed up or made a scandal, and who was a scallywag and why people thought so, who cheated and how everybody else's kopeks were spent. They talked freely even to a doctor about the woes of the soul, and before him they gave forth in the relaxation of spirit their terrific sighs—Lord, how the Russians sigh! But of their knowledge of political facts it was, and perhaps still is, hard to be sure. Possibly only when the situation is apt and the disclosure would clinch a point forcefully is their knowledge disclosed; but even then those who live under police must hesitate. At that time and place the people were their own police, their knowledge therefore was freed for public use.

MOUJIKS WANT GLASSES

THE FIRST Revolution which overthrew the Czar did not immediately affect the medical work in my village; but within a few months aged patients came complaining of symptoms quite unheard of among the villagers before. Presbyopia had not previously affected the daily life of the peasant as he did no near work; when he cut logs to build his house or sawed wood to make the window frames he did not measure closer than an inch. But now old men came to me with aching eyes; for they were learning to read now that they could do so without incurring the suspicion that they wanted to revolt. They borrowed school books and took instruction from their grandchildren. Of their land-hunger there had been much talk before the Revolution came, but I never guessed that the craving for learning would be so strong. It goes to show that when people are denied opportunity for self-development their true level cannot be judged while they are still under subjection. What these good souls got from their reading, their slow fingering of each word, each letter, was certainly but little of the author's meaning; no matter, they said, their children would learn quicker than they did, and in time all would read as freely as the priest.

When a priest moves among his flock he carries with him inevitably something of another life than this of ours on earth, so be he ever so human he always sees men as they think they ought to be. But in the great crises of life as well as in the vexing little ailments and injuries, the doctor is called in to help his patients to cling to this morsel of flesh, to get over painful times, and get deeper into the present with its everyday activities and its round of duties and cares. For this reason I found my opinion more often sought by the peasants than was that of the priest. His views coloured by his professional attitude to the future were, they felt, not as gross and earthly as theirs or mine.

Much of the aggressive element in the Russian disposition had, in the old régime, been turned inwards under the influence of an unusually mystical religion and an exceptionally autocratic régime, so that the people were submissive—not docile, that is too passive a concept—and unself-confident, but subject to outbursts of self-glorification and indignation against their oppressors. Furthermore, they were taxed so heavily that they spited their government by remaining poor. When I asked why, with their communal ownership of lands, they did not communally own a threshing-machine and so save themselves the back-breaking work with the flail or the wasteful treading of the grain by oxen, they answered that they would go on as they were doing rather than give the tax-gatherers the excuse to raise their dues because they could afford machinery.

It has puzzled many how the new régime acquired the power it wields over the minds of the people, since it first taxed the peasants as heavily as did Czardom and then liquidated them. Apart from the important fact that a majority of the present citizens of the Soviet Republic have never known another régime, I think the main source of its strength lies in the new direction given to the aggressive impulses of the people. When Lenin said 'Peasants! seize the land!' many of them had already done so; when the Bolsheviks said 'Workers, exploit your every opportunity!' the message did not fall on deaf ears. Work was to be their salvation and factories their new chapels; here they could pit themselves against materials they had hardly dared touch before, lest they call down on themselves an inquisition from the Governing Powers. The tax-greedy bureaucrats had stood between the energies of the people and the earth from which they derived both their life and their strength.

In another direction also the new régime met a need of the people. The Orthodox Church had in practice (I do not speak of the theory) two ways of dealing with the aggressive impulse; if turned outwards it must be at the service of the Czar and the State, but it was better to turn it against the self by fasts of inordinate length and most lowering to the physique (my Tartar patients were invariably fitter men at the time of spring ploughing than the Christians), and by a constant preoccupation with the worthlessness and wickedness of the self in wretched contrast to the ineffable glory and kindness of God.

The brutal anti-God campaign of the Bolsheviks was an endeavour to tap sources of energy of the people. Do not wallow in guilt and self-abnegation! they said in effect, there is nothing to fear but yourselves. Possess yourselves of Russia, master it by work, don't just pray for strength to overcome evil, work to make this land and this life better. For the first time the people were both appealed to and given a chance to turn their energies to constructive work. In the Czar's régime, taxation, which gave a minimum return in the way of social services—witness the scarcity of State doctors, in the country districts there were no others—and political oppression lowered the productive interests of the people and bred a hatred of the State. At the same time the hold of the Government was strengthened by suppressing education, freedom of movement, and the marketing of a man's own labour, and by using the Church as an auxiliary of the temporal power. But though the Bolsheviks pulled down the old gods they set up other gods in their places; the strong, half-Oriental, cynical portrait of Lenin, a Russian like themselves, was even in his lifetime offered for their worship and was accepted.

There can be no two opinions as to the extent of the change produced by the new religion of work and the new theology of dialectical materialism. The people were free to exploit their energies in a way undreamt of before. Gaffer comes for reading-glasses, the grandson goes to technical schools; the one has begun to give expression to his desire to know more of what is going on around him, the other to master a more complicated trade than his father—to become *skilled*. In the view of the new régime not only the wealth but also the happiness of the people depended on freedom to acquire and use skill. What applied to trades applied also to professions. Tens of thousands of 'medical assistants' were trained at short notice to bring medical help to the villages and towns. Their curriculum was sketchy but they were missionaries for better sanitation and a care for health. Only those who knew what conditions were like before should judge of the wisdom of that policy. It is not pleasant to think of the country being overrun by half-trained medical men, but they were better than gamps who used lamp-hooks on a retained placenta, and as the supply of better-trained doctors improved, these men could finish their studies.

The materialistic philosophy which guided the energies of the people to constructive work and to the acquisition of skill, and which therefore diminished the tendency to depression, introspection, and pessimism so common in the old régime in all classes of the community, may thus be said in a measure to replace the institutions which ministered to the spiritual needs of the people and furnished them with ideals. But the desire to employ science in the service of man is more readily fulfilled in the physical sciences than in the mental. It is easier to get men to improve their manual skill than it is to change their inner ways of thought.

The almost fantastic depths of self-abnegation and submission common in the days of the mystical Czardom is not in theory favoured as a national trait by materialist Commissars. But though, according to plan, the workers have risen in their pride, overthrown their oppressors, and asserted their rights as a free people, there is from time to time still an organized orgy of penitence—by proxy. In the State Trials the attitude of objectivity which characterizes so much of modern Russian life is laid aside and the accusers, the accused, and the 'organs of opinion' (the Press and the Platform) give themselves over to an exercise in moralizing and subjectivity that can only come from inner tension and self-distrust.

The service of the materialist revolutionaries has been great, they have opened out a new life to a people who were vilely oppressed, have raised them up and given them not only new hope but the means by which they can consolidate their gains; but the new materialist mode of thought has no rational way of dealing with the inner life of man. It denies the old gods and sets up new idols for worship. It lends the readiest ear to every discovery of science[1] except those which deal with the sufferings of the mind, and these it does not seem able to probe or even to acknowledge.

The Russian attitude towards feelings of guilt has always seemed strange alike to Western and Eastern peoples. In the religion of the old régime it was a central theme; in that of the new it is denied in relation to everything except the State. In the place of the old blasphemy —thoughts of hate against God and not believing in His goodness—there is now the sin of not believing in the perfect suitability of the present rulers and the present materialist philosophy for the needs of the Russian people. Discontent is taken as a sign of the unpardonable sin working in a diseased mind.

The materialism of the present rulers has put them into an awkward predicament; by attempting to eradicate every trace of superstition and bourgeois mentality and presenting the Socialist State and its founders as an

[1] Written in 1938.

object of adoration, they have given their people no alternative to either loving or hating the central power.

The psycho-analysts have pointed out one way in which the parliamentary government of Great Britain has overcome the problem: the constitution provides for a permanent or untouchable portion of the governing power (the king) and a removable portion (cabinet) which can be sacrificed without disturbing the loyalty to Authority. Thus discontent can find a safe outlet without disturbance or serious break in the function of government, and it is impossible for the executive to bedeck itself with the glamour of omnipotence and omniscience, which is always corrupting to wise judgment. Parliament may bestow enormous powers upon an individual for a special occasion, as in time of war or crisis: power thus freely *bestowed* implies the constraining force of a sense of responsibility. It is different when power is *seized*. Violence may be necessary in politics; but violence generates feelings of guilt which may be unconscious. It is foolish, and, I believe, in the long run politically imprudent, to deny a factor so important in mental —or political—life.

Every one of us in the village had mixed feelings on hearing of the fall of the Czar, nearly everyone rejoiced at the release from constraint, most of us felt that a great responsibility was laid upon us. Innocent though we were of the great political event, we felt obliged to shoulder the burden caused by our fantasied complicity in having desired it. The murder of the Czar deepened the sense of guilt because the image of the Little Father embodied a high ideal.

The Psychology of Great Russians
BY GEOFFREY GORER

CHAPTER I

CHILDHOOD TRAINING

I

IN COMPLEX societies, in which there is a hierarchy of social levels, anthropologists distinguish between 'class' societies and 'caste' societies. The distinction between caste and class is by no means clear-cut, and is indicated more by the relations between the groups than by the behaviour or composition of the groups themselves. In a class society the groups are typically in a single linear relation to one another from the upper to the lower and there is a general consensus as to which groups are superior and which inferior; if a person is socially mobile in a class society his mobility is through an orderly and predictable series of positions. In a caste society on the other hand the inter-relationship of the different groups is far more complex and relative superiority and inferiority are less clearly determined; social mobility (which occurs even in the most caste-bound societies) is less predictable, and does not necessarily follow an orderly sequence. Typically, members of caste societies have fewer feelings of inferiority than members of class societies; each caste has its defined role in the society and provides assurance and dignity for its members. In caste societies, much more than in class societies, a person's rights, privileges, duties, and in the vast majority of cases occupation, are determined by the group into which he is born; and it is unusual—often illegal—for a person to marry outside his or her caste. In caste societies it is general for each caste to develop its own customs, attitudes, and behaviour (in technical language its subculture) to a point of much greater contrast than is usual in class societies.

By all such criteria Great Russia was a caste society at least from the imposition of serfdom to its abandonment less than a century ago. Social mobility was possible through education, wealth or religious dedication, but this mobility was not progressive through a single line; it was not, for example, necessary to be a merchant before becoming a noble. Despite the great changes produced by the freeing of the serfs, the killing or exiling of most of the members of the existing upper castes after 1917, and the modifications in social structure produced by the changes of recent years, it still seems more accurate to treat Great Russia as a caste society. I shall therefore discuss the customs of child-rearing by caste.

2

The environment in which most Russian peasants live and work has probably changed very little in the thirty years since John Rickman was a country doctor among them. The climate certainly has not changed, nor the landscape; although electricity is available in some rural areas there is little reason to suppose the domestic architecture has changed, nor the general pattern of living. Most Russian peasants still lead extraordinarily isolated lives; few important new railway lines have been built in Great Russia, and there is an almost complete absence of usable motor roads, or of motors to travel on them if they existed. Communication is still almost entirely on foot or by horse-cart or sleigh.

Because of this static condition I am using the present tense to describe the customs of the Great Russian peasants, although the greater part of my most concrete material dates back twenty years or more. This is perhaps risky, and may describe the way in which the present generation of adults was reared, rather than the way they are rearing their children. I do know, however, that there have been no significant changes in those customs which are visible to an untrained observer.

From all the evidence we can get, it seems as though peasants accept the birth of a child as an inevitable portion of human life, rather than welcome it with very deep emotion. Parenthood does not seem to be psychologically necessary to Russian peasants to prove, or to complete, their masculinity or femininity; and it surely is not without significance that one of the most widely publicized transformations of the early revolution was the legalizing of abortions, and the sending out of propaganda trains and exhibitions on the right to abortion throughout the country. The later withdrawal of this right is congruent with the general withdrawal of the changes and privileges granted in the first years of the revolution; but it also suggests that perhaps excessive advantage was taken of it.

When a child is born it is normally very well treated, and protected from hunger, cold, and all other unpleasant physical experiences to the greatest possible extent, often at the cost of considerable parental sacrifice; but the attitude of the parents seems to be one of succouring protection, rather than of great emotional attachment.

Babies are fed by their mothers generously and frequently; whenever a baby cries the elders think that this means it is hungry. Normally a young peasant woman will be working in the fields within a relatively short time after having given birth; but she will return to the house or have the baby brought to her at frequent intervals. Russian women say that they know when the baby is hungry because their breasts ache; although this is physiologically accurate, I know of no other society which phrases the situation in the same way; and this can perhaps be interpreted as further evidence of the relative lack of deep emotional attachment to the child.

Apart from nursing, the baby is normally looked after by a woman of a generation older than the parents, typically a grandmother or great aunt, 'the old beldames who . . . in the management of infants hold absolute sway'. These old women are usually called *babushka* (grandmother) whether that is their actual relationship or no.[1] Sometimes older brothers and sisters also take a hand.

[1] On some few occasions throughout this study I have found it necessary to use Russian words, when no single English word or phrase will cover all the meanings. Thus, it is a saving of time to write

If the mother is on a journey or working in distant fields a comforter (called *nib*) is made for the baby; this consists of chewed-up food tied in a rag and fastened round the baby's neck. My informants said the food consisted of black bread among the poorer peasants, and white bread sweetened with sugar among the richer ones; but in the incident John Rickman describes it is bacon rind and baked flour. This might be a local variation, or something special for the baby's first food. If the baby cries while the mother is away, whoever is looking after it will moisten the *nib* with water if it has dried and then pop it in the baby's mouth, so that the baby is, as it were, plugged and cannot disturb the adults with its cries. Most of the time the baby is in a cradle attached to a springing ash-pole fixed to the ceiling or inner roof; unless it is born in early spring it is not taken outside the house for several months.

From the day of its birth onwards the baby is tightly swaddled in long strips of material, holding its legs

'*babushka*' rather than 'grandmother or great-aunt or some other old woman who may be more distantly related or not related at all'.

Russian is an inflected language, and changes the endings, and often the form of the words according to case, number, person, and tense, like Latin or German. I am following common anthropological custom and not inflecting the words: nouns are written in the nominative singular, and verbs in the infinitive, whatever position they hold in the sentence. Where nominal and verbal forms of the same root exist I am only employing one form. Since these words are used to illustrate an English text, it seems reasonable to use them as though they were English words.

It may be remarked that Russians normally add case-endings, &c., to English and American words and names when they use them in Russian sentences, despite the fact that English is relatively uninflected.

straight and its arms down by its sides. When Russians are asked why they swaddle their babies in this way, they give a considerable variety of reasons, but they all have one common theme: the baby is potentially so strong that if it were not swaddled it would risk destroying itself or doing itself irreparable harm, and would be impossible to handle. For one mother an unswaddled baby would risk developing a hunchback or crooked spine, others fear it would break its arms or legs or back by thrashing about, and would certainly have crooked limbs, others again that it would scratch out its eyes or ruin its nose. In the Ukraine (which of course may be different) in 1947 John Fischer was told by pediatricians, 'If a baby's hands were left untrammelled, he would wave them in front of his face, thus getting a fright which might permanently upset the nervous system'.[1] All Russians are agreed that an unswaddled baby is impossible to handle, and would jump out of constraining arms; Russians exposed to Occidental practices justified swaddling on the ground that Russians had no perambulators.

When swaddled the baby is completely rigid; one informant said the infants were like sticks, another likened them to sausages, a third to parcels. The baby can be held in any position and by any part of it without bending, and temporarily unswaddled infants are (according to the photographs) liable to maintain rigid poses which are very unusual in Occidental babies. The better the

[1] John Fischer, *Why They Behave Like Russians* (New York, 1947), p. 30; published in England under the title *The Scared Men in the Kremlin* (Hamish Hamilton).

mother, the firmer the bandages (the term which all my informants used for swaddling cloths): 'With a neat woman the bandages would be harder, because she would have prepared in advance and made double layers of cloth and sewn them together, closing down the ends. But with an untidy woman any old pieces of material would be used. But anyhow, I would say that they were harder than the napkins . . . which are wrapped round their legs and then tightly bound with strips of cloth to keep the legs straight so that they shouldn't bend.'

The usual method of swaddling is very impersonal and involves little contact between the baby and the swaddler. The infant is laid on its back on a table or other flat surface, and lifted from the ankles as the cloths are wrapped round. It seems possible that the concept of the baby's great and destructive strength is in some way communicated to the infant by the manner in which the adults handle it during the swaddling.

This swaddling is maintained on the average for about nine months though there may be variations according to the season. The baby is unswaddled, and wrapped in a loose shawl, for nursing unless the mother is too busy, and for occasional bathing in carefully adjusted tepid water, but for no other reason. In careful families the swaddling is removed gradually, the shoulders, chest, and arms being freed before the rest of the body; in more slatternly households all the swaddling is taken off at the same time. Informants say that the unswaddled baby crawls on all fours 'like a bear' before it can stand and walk.

Few other disciplines are put on the child before it can walk and talk. It is not expected to be clean before then; and later lapses are apparently treated lightly. We have very little information on infantile sexual play after the child is unswaddled (while it is swaddled there can obviously be none). The general picture seems to be that children are 'innocent' and 'sinless' and therefore nothing they can do can have any 'moral' or rather 'immoral' significance.

In most cases infants are nursed for a very considerable period, often up to two years or even more. This is done partly for reasons of economy—it is the cheapest way to feed a child—and partly as a device for postponing another pregnancy; the widely held belief that suckling prevents conception is subscribed to by the Great Russians. Even after the child has abandoned the breast as its major source of nourishment it will be allowed by its mother (if she has milk) to suckle occasionally, if it is frightened or disturbed or unwell. When the baby can sit up it is usually held on the knees of one of its parents during the adults' meal and is allowed to have a little of their food. Apart from their mothers' milk, children have exactly the same food as adults. This coarse fare may cause stomach-aches, and strong purges will be given to relieve these; purges are not reported as being normally given to relieve constipation.

Even before the child can speak it is likely to get its first training in the partly religious, partly magical, practices of Orthodox Christianity from the *babushka* looking after it; it will learn to prostrate itself, to make the sign of the cross to avert the evil spirits and dark forces which threaten to take possession of human beings; and, as it learns to speak, it will learn the ritual prayers. From about the age of five or six it partakes as fully in the ritual of the Orthodox Church as any layman, including confession and absolution.

This is not the place to discuss in any systematic way the many differences in dogma and ritual which contrast the Orthodox faith, as practised in Great Russia, with Roman Catholicism or other forms of Occidental Christianity. It is, however, necessary to describe Orthodox confession. The priest stands while the penitent kneels at his feet; the penitent makes a ritual statement of his great sinfulness, and the priest then cross-examines the penitent on his or her particular breaches of sin. Save in exceptional circumstances the penitent does not volunteer an account of what he thinks his sins are. With the belief in the universal sinfulness of human beings, it is not considered to be a lie to confess to sins one is not conscious of having committed; and priests may refuse absolution on the ground of contumely and spiritual pride if the penitent persists in denying sins of which his confessor accuses him. A number of Russians have told me of their first confession, and of how their parent or guardian instructed them to say 'I am guilty, father', every time the priest asked a question. Sometimes the children (perhaps not peasant children) did not know what the priest was referring to; in most such cases the priest would pass on quickly.

At the end of confession most penitents are in a highly emotional state, weeping and beating their foreheads; the priest may impose penances of fasts or other mortifications of the flesh; he then covers the penitent kneeling at his feet with the lappets of his ritual garment and pronounces the absolution.

Absolution gives a feeling of great psychological relief, and is very highly valued by most people. In a way, absolution seems to give a retrospective justification to sin; as a widely quoted proverb says: 'If you do not sin, you cannot repent.' Many Russians state that repentance is more highly to be esteemed than innocence; and this although uncontaminated 'innocence' in adults is valued and respected.

Great Russian peasants cleanse their bodies too, at regular intervals—usually once a week—in the village steam-baths, during which the body is violently purged of all impure matters by great heat. Young children go with their mothers; from about the age of five little boys go with their fathers and elder brothers. The glow—partly physical and partly psychological—which follows this cleansing is highly valued.

When small peasant children gain complete physical control they contribute to the household by doing various odd jobs, including on occasion looking after their younger brothers and sisters. The chief demand which adults make on young children is that they shall not be a nuisance; if they do become so, or if the father is drunk, they may get severely thrashed. It is important to note that such punishments are capricious. The child 'is slapped not for his own good, but because the grown-up was annoyed'. Such punishments are likely to be spasmodically administered, and the community will not stand for their being too severe or frequent; I have a number of stories of villagers reprimanding a father who thrashed his sons too much.

In many ways the whole village community is likely to be treated by the young child as though it were a single extended family. A child will play with all the children of its own age and will be as free to enter other houses or gardens as those of its parents; it will receive from the neighbours the same kind of emotionally calm succour and food as it would do at home.

The normal relationships between parents and children would seem to be of low intensity. The child owes complete obedience, gratitude, and respect to his parents; and the parents, especially perhaps the father, get satisfaction from the child's growing strength and capacities. Childish precocity—the time at which children acquire new skills—is not valued, and there does not seem to be even a common Russian word to describe it.

The relationship between brothers and sisters would appear to be normally friendly and of the low intensity usual in Russian family relationships, on condition that they be equally treated by the adults and of more or less the same capacities. If one child is markedly more gifted or more favoured than his brothers or sisters, there is likely to be considerable resentment on the part of those who feel themselves disadvantaged. As the proverb says: 'If a son is cleverer than his father there is joy, but if one brother is cleverer than another there is jealousy.'

Russian peasants do not seem to feel any fear that a boy or girl will not fulfil its sex role adequately, and there is no record of anxiety being demonstrated if for a time children play with toys or engage in occupations more customary for the opposite sex. In adult life, the occupations of peasant men and women are generally different; but if unusual circumstances compel a man to do a woman's work or vice versa he or she is not thought to have lost dignity or status thereby. Women are felt to be strong; men's larger frames and bigger muscles may give individuals greater physical strength, but the difference is purely physical.

In the first years after the Revolution the Soviet government made considerable propaganda in favour of the type of child-training then current in the West (particularly the United States); but as far as the peasants in the villages were concerned, the only major change seems to have been some increase of attention to hygiene—for example, sterilizing the rag in which the comforter was wrapped, washing hands, and boiling drinking water—and earlier recourse to medically qualified people if the children got ill. During the period of active anti-religious propaganda—roughly from 1923 to 1940—participation in Church rituals was obviously limited, and some secrecy may have been necessary in the teaching of religion. The large crowds of young soldiers present at Church services after the ban was lifted—a fact recorded by many witnesses—suggest strongly that such instruction continued to be given. Many more children than before 1917 attend school between the ages of seven and fourteen.

3

Before 1917, there were very few factory workers whose parents had been factory workers also in Great Russia outside St. Petersburg and Moscow.[1] The great number of urban workers were reared as peasants, and in many cases they returned to their villages to marry and raise their children. Where children were born to urban workers they were (it would seem) raised on the same principle as peasants' children, though possibly less attention was paid in some cases to their religious instruction.

With the increase of industrialization under the Soviets, the number and proportion of children born to urban workers has greatly increased; and this is the group which the innovations of government policy and government-sponsored practice have the most influenced, with the possible exception of the large group of lesser government employees, about whom we have regrettably no knowledge.

In the cities expectant mothers are meant to attend clinics to receive proper medical instruction during their pregnancy and to get advice on the treatment of the young child. Owing to the general overcrowding (even by Russian standards) workers' babies are generally born in hospital, though the lying-in period is usually less than a week; and mothers are meant to consult clinicians

[1] There were probably more 'hereditary' workers in other portions of the Russian empire: the Black Sea ports, especially Odessa, Baku, Kiev, &c.

about their infants' treatment at regular intervals. Particularly in the earlier years of the Soviet régime, and to a modified extent even to-day, the advice which the clinicians gave was in line with current American practice, and against the traditional Russian customs: they advocated scheduled nursing, early toilet training, light and unhampering infant's clothes. The way the advice was treated is exemplified by the remarks of one Russian mother who brought up her two children in Moscow in the late twenties and thirties, and who was very active in kindergartens, parent-teacher associations, and so on:

'Officially babies shouldn't be swaddled, and all sorts of explanations were given as to why it was better not to be, but nearly all the babies I saw were swaddled. The mothers were so busy they had to make the child secure. You know they didn't have anything like straps or leading-strings. In order to keep the babies safe even my intellectual friends would swaddle their children. You know there are no prams in Russia and people had to carry their babies, and it's much easier to carry a swaddled child. And then you know it's cold in Russia and swaddling the child keeps the baby warm. Teachers used to teach mothers that it was bad to swaddle the children and that they would develop much better muscles if their limbs were free; they tried to teach more modern ways. In the exhibitions there were pictures of the clothing children should wear, but nearly every baby I saw was swaddled. . . .

'The young mothers that I knew accepted the propaganda against swaddling but explained why they did the opposite. In the same way modern theory said that you shouldn't pick up a child when it cries and carry it around all the time. The mothers said: "What can we do? If the child cries, it will disturb the neighbours." Or another gave the story of how her husband had to have quiet in the house. This treatment of the children and why they couldn't follow the theory was a constant subject of conversation. . . .

'Mothers were told that they should feed their children regularly, but they didn't have time for this and didn't know about calories and vitamins. They were told they should feed them every three or four hours. But many mothers couldn't do this because conditions did not permit this. Mothers had to feed their children lest they cry and disturb the neighbours. Russians like their children very much and like to do this because they thought this would be the way to save the new generation. . . .

'There is a good deal of propaganda to train [for cleanliness] early in life; the Russians advocated it strongly. But mothers didn't have the time, or the possibility to do it and so they did very little. They left the children to themselves. Of course it was different in the government nurseries. There they were trained early and fed on schedule, but at home mothers don't do that. . . .

'Most of the mothers I'm talking about were a very loyal Soviet generation, and they didn't feel guilty [about not following the government rules] because life was so hard for them. They didn't feel any personal guilt. I remember one mother telling me that she was bringing up her children in the old way because they were living in such crowded conditions, but if they got more room in a few years she would treat the children differently.'

Because of her professional interest in child-care and education, this woman is a particularly reliable witness; and what she says is borne out by the other informants who have lived in Great Russian towns in recent years. Unless the mother worked in a factory which had a day nursery of adequate size and equipment (and this is still

fairly uncommon) most workers' children were and are
brought up in their earliest years in much the same way
as peasant children.

The Soviets have established a legal holiday for a
newly delivered mother; when that is up the mother
normally returns to work and the baby is usually looked
after by a *babushka*. The mother is meant to be given intervals for nursing the baby, either returning home for
the purpose or the baby being brought to her. Many city
babushka trained their charges in religious ritual; but
there was much more militant atheism among the
workers.

For most workers' children who have passed infancy
the role of religion in the old régime is now replaced by
the teachings and practices of communism. Nursery
school and kindergarten space is planned for all workers'
children and is probably already available for a large
number; and in them supervised games, occupations,
songs, and stories start instilling the approved attitudes
and beliefs. The mother I quoted before told me:

'Children go to kindergarten from the age of three
and a half; that is where it's possible; in Moscow many
wanted to and could not because there was no room.
But there are other institutions which take care of children when both parents work. In kindergarten they
begin to get a complete Soviet ideological education. I
remember a children's camp in the summer of 1929,
when the collectivization propaganda was going on. The
kindergartens and summer camps got a directive, as it
was called, to explain collectivization to the children; we
mothers were indignant about it (a thing we couldn't
have done later) and they asked me, as I was chairman,

to protest. Well, one day there was a programme devoted to collectivization. I saw they were doing a marvellous job. They made sand games for the children, showing how they could do much more if they would work together; and I made a report that there was nothing to get indignant about. Of course, they made the children repeat a lot of hard words they didn't understand; but when a child leaves kindergarten he is quite an enlightened little Soviet citizen and full of devotion for his country.'

Besides kindergartens, there are supervised playgrounds attached to many of the big apartment houses, and in Moscow on the outer boulevards. Patriotic holidays are much used to drive home ideological lessons. From the age of seven children go to school and belong to the 'Pioneers', the communist organization for the young folk.

One of the areas in which there have been the most violent oscillations of Soviet policy is the officially approved attitude towards parents and teachers. A young woman who first went to school in Moscow in 1921 said:

'In Moscow in 1921 there was a positive Soviet approach. There were no melancholy poems read. I was nine and we were left alone. We worked on the Dalton plan. The teacher had no authority whatsoever. We were broken into units of four or five of our own choosing. . . .

'The children in school all had the feeling that they couldn't rely on their families. There was no such thing. The government encouraged it and said it was the government who was supposed to take care of the children. We were completely liberated from our parents. We felt no responsibility to them.'

As her education progressed, Soviet policy changed; by 1928 or 1929

'the teacher's authority became greater and greater. . . . As time went on—my later experiences in school—the political situation changed and it became something that was imposed on you. The democratic method [of choosing student representatives] was abolished. The representatives of the Party were assigned to the school. There were lists of selected people from whom you could choose. . . . The third year [1931] they didn't let them choose but appointed a boy instead of me.'

During about the first ten years of the Soviet régime, parents had legally no authority over their children, and children were not meant to have any respect for their parents. Children could complain to the school and party authorities if their parents punished them; and then the parents would be punished in their turn, if they had disciplined their children for any reason except the infraction of the rules of the school or the Pioneers. These attitudes towards parent-child relationships were changed in the thirties; by about 1936 parents were made responsible for their children's delinquencies, even if these had occurred away from the parents' supervision, for example, if boys spoiled public property or engaged in any acts of hooliganism.

The most recent expression of the official attitudes that I know of is found in a text-book issued for teachers in 1946:

'The feeling of love for father and mother is the first noble feeling which arises naturally in a child and which plays a central role in the life of every individual. . . . Our children must appreciate how honourable is the title of mother in our land. Only in the Soviet Union has the state established the title of "Mother-heroine" and the bestowal of orders and medals on mothers of many children. And with the word "father" we address the Great Stalin when we wish to express to him the feeling of filial nearness, and of love and respect. . . . In our country there are no conflicts between fathers and children. . . .'[1]

4

Although most of the members of the former upper castes—the greater and lesser nobility and the merchants —seem to have been either killed or exiled in 1917 and the years following, it is perhaps of interest to describe briefly the way in which they were brought up; this may explain some of the points of contrast with the behaviour of the present upper castes.

Whether an upper-caste mother nursed her baby or not was a question of fashion and individual temperament. In the first years of the twentieth century there was a more general tendency for such mothers to nurse their own babies; for those who did so, it was a very great tie, for the babies were fed every two hours during the day and for many months. During the nineteenth century nearly all upper-caste babies were suckled by peasant wet-nurses, *kormilitsa*; and in the twentieth

[1] D. P. Yesipov and N. K. Goncharov, *Pedagogy* (Moscow, 1946). Partly translated and edited by George S. Counts and Nucia P. Lodge under the title *I Want To Be Like Stalin* (New York, John Day, 1947, and London, Gollancz, 1948), pp. 72–5.

century this was still very general. These wet-nurses were either poor women or unmarried mothers. It was very rare for the *kormilitsa* to be allowed to nurse her own child as well; it was feared that either she would favour her own child over the foster-child, or that she would be anxious concerning her own child and so 'turn' her milk. There was consequently no expected relationship between foster-children, such as is found in other societies.

In looking for a wet-nurse it was essential to find one whose own child was exactly the same age as the foster-child, but the relative sexes were not considered. It was believed that these wet-nurses' milk would 'turn' or dry up very easily if the nurse became angry or disaffected or jealous; and consequently they were greatly indulged and their whims were attended to promptly. They were provided with the colourful 'national' Russian costumes which are to-day so regularly featured in night-clubs and musical comedies in Great Britain and the United States.

Apart from the actual nursing (whoever did this) the child would be looked after by an old and experienced peasant woman called *nyanya*. *Nyanya* normally only had complete control over the infant during its first two years; but in many households the *nyanya* was permanent, looking after each child in turn, and frequently going on to the second generation. In such cases *nyanya* was often the chief authority in the household; I have stories of married men, fathers of families, being scolded by their old *nyanya* and meekly doing their bidding. *Nyanya* were expected to be temperamental, to be swept by unaccounted-for moods; mothers would tell their children to respect such moodiness. On rare occasions men would play the role of *nyanya*, especially orderlies in military families, and sometimes devoted family servants.

In contrast to peasant children, upper-caste children were *always* expected to be unswaddled for nursing; and they were usually left unswaddled for half an hour before the evening bath when they could kick and exercise their limbs. After about 1900 a new style of wrapping up children became fashionable: they were put in 'envelopes'—large squares of material stuffed with down and typically quilted, which were fastened over both sides and from the bottom; the child's head and neck were supported by a pillow. This style allowed the child a little lateral movement of its limbs.

Most upper-caste children learned religious observances and beliefs from *nyanya*. It is very uncommon to find Russians who have clear memories of their early childhood; the few I did elicit dwelt on such subjects:

'Old *nyanya* was very religious, and there was always a fire in front of the ikon, and old *nyanya* used to pray for a long time and speak in words we couldn't understand, and she'd pray and bow down and pray and then go to bed herself. It was very, very peaceful.'

'The old *nyanya* used to place the child and point the ikon out to it from the word go. *Bog* [God] is among the first words the child learns to speak, and often the children could point to the picture of God before they could say a word. And then in each room there's the ikon with the lamp in front of it and the child sees the *nyanya* praying and bowing.'

All castes in Russia tend to connect Christianity with

the peasantry. Peasants typically described themselves, and were referred to, as 'Christians'.

Another very important part of the *nyanya's* function was quieting and entertaining her charges with the traditional folk-tales and songs. Russians regularly repeat the fact that Pushkin learned his wonderful stories from his old *nyanya*.

From the age of two or three, and often till they had passed adolescence, upper-caste children were put in the charge of a variety of maids, governesses, and tutors of almost any Occidental nationality except Russian, often two or three at a time, to teach them manners and various accomplishments, especially foreign languages. These foreign instructors were frequently changed. As soon as a child's table manners were good enough it would eat with its parents, except on formal occasions; and in most houses children were free to go anywhere provided they did not disturb the grown-ups. Russian upper-caste children spent most of their waking life in those rooms from which the adults were temporarily absent, or out of doors.

Like peasant children, most upper-caste children grew up in the emotional equivalent of a very large family; though in their case blood kinship often played a more important role. In the towns relatives usually lived very close together, often having flats in the same buildings as their parents or married brothers or sisters; in the country summer-long visits were paid by whole families of relations. In the bigger households it was customary for there to be permanent additions in the shape of more distant poor or unmarried relatives and other dependants, who stood in a quasi-parental role to the child. In the case of families living isolated in the country with few children of their own caste it was customary to choose some of the peasant children from the village to be educated with the upper-caste children. The happiest childhood recollection reported by upper-caste men who were educated in the country is playing with the peasant boys, away from the supervision of governesses and tutors.

The chief contrasts so far discovered between the typical experiences of children from the upper castes and from the peasant caste seem to have been the following: upper-caste children were not expected to manifest responsibility or to contribute early to the comfort or wealth of the household; and the presence of governesses and tutors of non-Russian culture often produced emotional conflicts, either by their demands, their attitudes or their sudden removal, which accentuated tendencies in later life to neuroses and character problems similar to those found in Occidental society, and different in form and content from those found among Russians not early exposed to non-Russian influence.

Officers can be considered a sub-caste of the upper caste, for the profession was in the great number of cases hereditary; there were special military schools exclusively for officers' children.[1] Officers tended to be poorer than the majority of the upper caste and to have smaller families. Orderlies often acted as *nyanya*.

[1] It is interesting to note that such schools were recently re-established in the U.S.S.R.

5

One of the most exclusive castes in pre-revolutionary Russia was the 'white' priests, the Orthodox priests who married and did most of the parish work; the higher ranks in the hierarchy were filled by the 'black' priests, who had taken a vow of celibacy, and might be recruited from any caste. By ecclesiastical law priests were only allowed to marry priests' daughters; their elder sons had to become priests, but in large families—and priests' families were normally very large, for there were state bounties for children—younger sons would go into other professions, especially teaching.

'White' priests were considered 'outsiders' by the upper castes and peasants alike. In the villages priests ran the parochial schools, and their children would mingle with the peasant children during school hours; they seem to have had little contact with them or with other adults apart from this. Most 'white' priests were poor, and only had such domestic help as their straitened means allowed. Many 'white' priests were ignorant men.

6

I have not been able to get any concrete information on the methods of bringing up children customary to the caste called *meshchanye*—the '*petite bourgeoisie*', the small shopkeepers and white-collar workers, the stewards and overseers who play so large a role in many of the best-known Russian plays and novels. In the present régime their place seems to have been taken by the lesser government employees and bureaucrats; for that caste too I have no concrete information.

7

The castes so far described compose a stable society; the members of each caste have their probable life and occupation marked out for them from birth. What happens when an individual, through temperament or individual gifts, feels himself unsuited for life in his caste?

Till the beginning of the nineteenth century there was only one way of life outside the castes open: religious dedication as a 'black' priest or nun, whether for study or contemplation in the monasteries and convents, or, for men, in the upper hierarchy of the Orthodox Church, or in one of the numerous schismatic sects. 'Black' priests took a vow of celibacy (if the vocation came after marriage they renounced their families), and consequently the group did not perpetuate itself.

From about 1820 onwards[1] there developed an alternative career for those whose talent, interests or temperament rendered them ill at ease in the conventional

[1] The following statements are chiefly founded on D. N. Ovsianiko-Kulikovsky's exhaustive *History of the Russian Intelligentsia* (St. Petersburg, 1914, 3 vols.).

life of their castes; this was the study and practice of science, technology, and the arts as they had developed in Western Europe. A number of individuals acquired these techniques with varying efficiency; there was, however, no place in the existing Russian society for them, and they gradually formed a predominantly urban group on the edge of the Russian caste system—if the habitual overtones of the term can be forgotten they could properly be described as 'out-castes'—which was later labelled the intelligentsia.

The intelligentsia were always a very small group numerically[1] but their influence, both inside and outside Russia, can hardly be overestimated. With few exceptions, the writers and musicians of the latter half of the nineteenth century and after come from this group, and they are consequently almost completely responsible for the views on Russia held by non-Russians.

Whatever their views or pursuits, the intelligentsia differed from their compatriots by the fact that they abandoned the automatic, almost unconscious, following of traditional Russian culture; they questioned current Russian behaviour in the light of the contrasts which

[1] Russian authorities differ on the way the intelligentsia should be counted. One of the favourite occupations of the intelligentsia was an attempt to define itself and number its members. One of them, Pyshekhonov, in his *Materials for the Characterization of Social Relationships in Russia* (St. Petersburg, 1904), maintains that the best way to count them is by the signatures received when some famous member of their group is honoured. At Mikhalovsky's jubilee 20,000 signatures were received in this way. The all-Russian census of 1897, published in 1905, lists something under 200,000 for all the members of the 'intelligent' professions, including their households, for the whole of Russia.

they established with Western Europe; and they claimed the moral autonomy of judging their own society. From their origin, and to this day, the intelligentsia have been divided into 'Westernizers' and 'Slavophiles'; but the latter, no less than the former, are influenced in their judgements and attitudes by the impact of alien (Occidental) cultures.

Like the 'black' priests, the intelligentsia were recruited from all castes, on the basis of education, talents, and individual temperament; possibly the children of the lesser nobility and of the 'white' priests contributed the greatest number. As with the religious vocation, membership of the intelligentsia separated the individual from the emotionally large and extended families in which most Great Russians lived all their lives. But unlike the black priests, the intelligentsia married and had children.

The children of the intelligentsia were born into a setting which contrasted sharply with that of the 'caste' Russians; instead of spreading their emotions over a great number of adults and children they were most of them reared in small families, their most constant adult contacts being with their parents, and among children with their own brothers and sisters.

Together with other 'Westernizing' ideas the intelligentsia imported (at least, to the best of their ability) Occidental ideas of the proper way to bring up children. The children of the intelligentsia were not, as a rule, swaddled; older informants will explain, 'We were not swaddled because we belonged to the intelligentsia'. In most such families the mothers looked after their babies themselves, or had trained foreign nurses or governesses, and imposed feeding schedules and earlier cleanliness training. In many families the children did not receive conventional religious instruction.

The leading members of the various clandestine revolutionary parties were drawn almost entirely from the intelligentsia; the schools and universities were the chief recruiting ground for this group: for many adolescents conspiratorial politics played a role analogous to sexual experimentation in the West. In the vast majority of cases where one can trace the social development of Lenin's colleagues and collaborators—the 'professional revolutionaries'—they came from the same 'out-caste' group.

When the 'professional revolutionary' section of the intelligentsia achieved supreme power after 1917, they immediately instituted propaganda (as has already been pointed out) for contemporary Occidental-style pediatrics; all the traditional Russian methods of child-rearing were inveighed against; in this, as in all other spheres, the U.S.S.R. was going to 'equal and eventually surpass' the West. Despite the current Slavophile repudiation of the West in most other spheres, these attitudes to (relative) bodily freedom, scheduled nursing, and very early toilet training are still favoured and practised in the best state crèches and children's homes, if one can judge by the photographs and the pamphlets and brochures. It seems reasonable to suppose that these approved 'modern' and 'scientific' practices are followed in the families of the present Soviet élites.

Detailed analysis of the photographs of children in

crèches shows that there are some significant differences between Soviet and Western practices; hand-mouth exploration is considerably impeded, and various devices isolate the child from its environment, its fellows, and the adults to an extent which is not customary elsewhere.

CHAPTER II

CHARACTER DEVELOPMENTS

I

THIS CHAPTER will be occupied by a description of what appear to be some of the typical characteristics of the majority of what may be called 'caste' Great Russians. Nothing which follows is meant to apply to any other of the societies of the U.S.S.R.; unless explicitly stated otherwise, it also does not apply to the *children* of the intelligentsia or of the Soviet élites, nor to children raised in institutions. I have not been able to study enough of these 'out-castes' to discover any positive regularities in their childhood experience; they are united negatively in not sharing—at least with any completeness—the earliest experiences of the majority of their compatriots.

2

Under normal conditions the Russian infant is not exposed to conditions which might be expected to give rise to any of the painful internal physiological feelings which often form part of the infantile experience of members of other societies. He is not expected to be

hungry or cold, and no demands for the control of elim-
ination direct his early attention on his gastro-intestinal
tract. But except during the short periods when he is
being fed or bathed he is completely inhibited in the free
movement of his limbs; he cannot explore the external
universe through the use of his hands or through carrying things to his mouth; the only way he can express
emotion of any sort is through his eyes or by screaming;
and the latter may be impeded by 'plugging' the baby
with the comforter.

These facts are observable and verifiable; their inci-
dence could easily be established statistically. The deductions which follow are unverified hypotheses, though
verification could be obtained.

When human infants are not constrained they move
their limbs and bodies a great deal, especially during the
second six months of life; it seems probable that much
of this movement is physiologically determined, as an
aspect of biological maturation. Infants tend to express
emotion with their whole body and not merely their
face, for example arching their back or thrashing about
or hugging. They also explore their own body and the
universe around them with their hands and their mouth,
gradually discovering what is edible and what inedible,
what me and what not-me. While they are swaddled in
the Russian manner, Russian infants can do none of
these things; and it is assumed that this inhibition of
movement is felt to be extremely painful and frustrating
and is responded to with intense and destructive rage,
which cannot be adequately expressed physically. This
rage, it is assumed, is directed at the constraint, rather

than at the people who constrain the infant. Since the infant's exploration of the universe is very limited it would seem that the identification of the people who constrain him is impeded; the more so since, as has already been pointed out, the actual swaddling is done in a very impersonal manner with little contact between the swaddler and the infant who is handled and turned around almost as though it were a rigid and inanimate object.

Teething normally starts while the infant is still swaddled; and evidence from Occidental children shows that this is usually a physiologically and psychologically important aspect of their development. It therefore seems probable that fantasies of biting and destroying by devouring play a major part in the hypothecated rage. Partial confirmation of the important psychological role of teeth and biting can be found from a number of sources. Russian folklore contains the figure (which I do not know of in any other folklore) of the Witch Baby with the Iron Teeth who devours her parents,[1] as well as the more common old witch Baba Yaga who also has iron teeth. In Russian swearing and invective animals with prominent teeth and tusks (hyenas, jackals, sealions, crocodiles, dogs, &c.) play a major and consistent role; Soviet propaganda frequently described the Nazis (and subsequently their later enemies) as cannibalistic. I have the impression that in Russian political caricatures hostile figures are drawn with exaggeratedly large teeth.

[1] Older ballet-goers may remember the figure of the witch baby in the Diaghilev ballet *Contes d'Enfants*, frighteningly mimed by Lydia Sokolova.

It is perhaps relevant that the Soviet dental service provides false teeth of stainless steel.

Psychoanalysis has coined the phrase 'omnipotence of thought' to describe the typical mental processes of infants and young children before they can distinguish between wish and reality. If this is the case the assumed destructive rage would appear to give the infant a feeling of overwhelming destructive strength; and this may well be one of the sources for the rationalizations given by adults for swaddling their children.

A second very primitive thought mechanism is technically known as 'projection'; this is acting as though the thoughts or wishes emanating from the self (whether conscious or unconscious) were emanating from persons other than the self. It is assumed that this mechanism is regularly employed by Great Russian infants who project on to the vague figures in their environment their own hostile wishes; in consequence they feel that they risk being bitten or devoured if they were to gratify their destructive wishes (or in retaliation for having gratified them in fantasy). It is worth noting that swaddling prevents the gross muscular movements of the limbs which accompany 'temper tantrums' in unswaddled children; and as a consequence fantasies of rage and destruction will not normally be accompanied by fantasies which involve the voluntary use of the large muscles. This may help account for the emphasis given by many Russians to the workings of the soul and the inner nature.

Because of this projection of their hostility and fear the painful restraints which exacerbate the destructive rage become at the same time an essential protection both for the Russian infants themselves and for those around them; for the restraint prevents the full gratification of the destructive wishes, and so saves the infants from the fantasied perils of retaliation.

It would appear that Russian adults generally do little or nothing to an older child in a rage or temper tantrum; but it is worth noting that Russian adults, though normally so impervious to outside disturbances, appear to feel very great discomfort at infantile screams, and feel that their fellows would be equally disturbed. Since adult intervention would appear to be limited to quieting the screaming infant by 'plugging' it with the comforter, it would seem that infants sometimes exhaust themselves physically and psychologically with unassuaged rage. This exhaustion to the point of impotence would seem to be accompanied by feelings of complete loneliness and helplessness. This feeling of impotent exhaustion would appear to be an analogue to the state of *depression* described in adult melancholics.[1]

If this depression is the nadir of infantile misery, then all other emotions and experiences, however relatively unpleasant, gain some positive value as a sign that one is 'alive', not overwhelmed with weakness, helplessness,

[1] I developed this hypothetical linking of swaddling and the 'depressive position' of infants, as described by Mrs. Klein, on the basis of literary material quoted and analysed by Dr. N. Leites after I had left the United States and written my first formulations on Great Russian character. (See Appendix I, p. 218). I should like to express my sense of indebtedness to Dr. Leites for this material, as well as for much other assistance in the course of this study. I understand that Dr. Leites is preparing a study of Bolshevism.

loneliness; even the rage which is presumed to precede, and probably to follow, the attack of depression becomes also positively valued. A symbolic illustration of these feelings may be found in a lyric written by Pushkin in 1830 entitled *Imps of Hell* (*Bjessy*).

Storm clouds are dashing on, storm clouds are whirling, the invisible moon lights up the flying snow. The sky is opaque, the night is opaque. I am driving, driving in the wide open field. The sleigh-bell goes din, din, din. Against my will I am afraid amidst the unknown plains.

'Hey, go ahead, driver.'

'It is impossible to bear it, it is hard on the horses, master. The snow storm sticks together my eyes, all the roads are swept by snow. May I be killed, but no tracks can be seen; we went astray, what should we do? The imp of hell leads us, it seems, and makes us circle in all directions. Look—there, there he plays—he blows and spits on me! Now he pushes into the ravine the horse that got wild! There he stuck before me like a non-existing mile-post, there he flashed like a small spark, and disappeared in the empty darkness!'

Storm clouds are dashing, storm clouds are whirling, the invisible moon lights up the flying snow. The sky is opaque, the night is opaque.

We have no strength any more to circle around. The sleigh-bell, all of a sudden, becomes silent, the horses stop. What is it there in the field? A stump or a wolf?

The snow storm is cruel, the snow storm is crying, the sensitive horses are snorting. There he jumps—only the eyes are burning in the mist.

The horses again tear away, the sleigh-bell din, din, din. I see the spirits gather amidst the whitened plains. Endless, ugly, in the opaque play of the moon, all kinds of imps twirl around, like leaves in November.

How many of them are there? Where are they driven? What are they singing so plaintively? Are they burying the house spirit, or marrying off a witch?

Storm clouds are dashing, storm clouds are whirling. The

invisible moon lights up the flying snow. The sky is opaque, the night is opaque. The devils are dashing, swarm after swarm, in the limitless height. With their plaintive yelps and howls they wound my heart.[1]

It seems probable that, using the mechanism of projection, the infant considers that these depressions are produced by the external world, possibly as retaliation for his hostile wishes; and, as will be developed later, an unconscious fear of a return to such a state remains operative in adult life.

These feelings of rage and fear are probably made endurable, but also given emphasis, by the fact that the baby is periodically loosed from the constraints, and suckled and petted while unswaddled. This alternation of complete restraint without gratifications, and of complete gratifications without restraint, continues for at least the first nine months of life. It is the argument of this study that the situation outlined in the preceding paragraphs is *one* of the major determinants in the development of the character of adult Great Russians.[2]

It is *not* the argument of this study that the Russian manner of swaddling their children produces the Rus-

[1] Cf. the behaviour of the peasant in 'Snow', p. 40.

[2] I should like to stress as forcibly as possible that I consider the hypothesized derivatives from swaddling as only one of a presumably large number of antecedents to the development of Great Russian character. Further investigations would almost certainly develop others of similar importance. The vulgarizations and misinterpretations of my paper 'Themes in Japanese Culture' (*Transactions of the New York Academy of Sciences*, New York, March 1943, and *Penguin Science News No.* 1, London, 1945) have falsely imputed to me a belief in a monistic antecedent to Japanese adult character. I trust that a similar error will not be committed in the present instance.

sian character; and it is not intended to imply that Russian character would be changed or modified if some other technique of infant training were adopted. Swaddling is one of the devices which Russian adults employ to communicate with the child in its first year of life, to lay the foundation for those habits and attitudes which will subsequently be developed and strengthened by all the major institutions in Great Russian society. It was through the study of swaddling practices that I discovered what appear to me to be some of the most important clues to the interpretation of Russian behaviour;[1] and the derivatives of the swaddling situation became for me as it were the thread which led through the labyrinth of the apparent contradictions of adult Russian behaviour. The thread is not the labyrinth; but it is psychologically almost impossible for the explorer, who has relied on a thread, not to over-emphasize its importance. Individuals have a childhood, but society does not; child-training practices are one of the devices through which a culture is maintained through time.

3

For several months, at least, the Russian infant experiences intense but relatively undirected rage and fears deriving from his projection of this rage on to the external world; as a result of this he develops a feeling of pervasive though unfocused guilt. So pervasive is

[1] See Appendix I.

this unfocused guilt for some Russians that they can (or did) feel responsible for the sins and miseries of the whole world, an emotion most graphically and beautifully described by Dostoievsky in his major novels. This feeling of diffuse guilt presumably underlies the Orthodox dogma of the universal sinfulness of human beings, and accounts for the admission in confession of sins one is not conscious of having committed; it would also help account for the great feeling of psychological relief which accompanies confession and absolution for the devout, and also for the role which confessions outside religion have continuously played in Russian public life. The sensational confessions of the purge trials of 1936–8 and the recantations of error in communist self-criticism are modern examples; an older example, dating from 1892, comes from one of the most hostile critics of Czarist Russia, E. B. Lavrin:

'Nothing is more striking or characteristic in the annals of Russian criminal justice than the almost mathematical certainty with which one can predict that a person arrested on suspicion, even though there be no legal proofs of guilt, and no likelihood of their ever being obtained, will take the Juge d'Instruction into his confidence and glibly relate every detail of his share in the transaction. Out of sixty-five criminal cases taken at random, I find that in forty-eight the prisoners were convicted on their own confession, and in most of the remainder there was no need for self-accusation, as the malefactors were caught red-handed.'[1]

[1] E. B. Lavrin, *Russian Characteristics* (London, Chapman & Hall, 1892), p. 115. 'E. B. Lavrin' is the pseudonym of the *Times* correspondent of the period, Dr. Dillon.

Although I have described the general Russian feeling of responsibility for evil and apprehension of punishment as 'guilt' it is important to bear in mind that this 'guilt' is of a different nature to that commonly manifested by the members of Occidental Protestant cultures. In the Occident guilt-feelings apparently become formalized considerably later in life, and are perceived as fear of punishment from specific external (or later internalized) parental or quasi-parental figures for having contravened specific ethical rules.[1] Among the Great Russians, however, these guilt-feelings apparently arise before people in the external world are clearly differentiated, and indeed before the acquisition of adequate speech, and are felt, not as fear of punishment from specific figures, but as fear of dark forces (*tyomniye sili*) which might overwhelm one. These dark forces might arise either inside or outside the individual.

The common practice of Orthodox Christianity made this fear concrete as the fear of possession by an evil spirit or devil who would take up its abode in a person's heart; and there were a number of ritual practices designed to avert this psychic disaster. Many children, for example, were taught to make the sign of the cross over their mouths every time they yawned; should they fail to do so, the lurking evil spirit would jump through their mouths into their hearts. The extent of these fears can be illustrated by the reminiscences of a young woman, who

[1] The internalized figures, with their autonomous control over the ego's behaviour, are termed by the psychoanalysts the super-ego. The portion of the super-ego which is available to consciousness corresponds to the 'conscience' of popular and religious parlance.

was looked after by a *nyanya* when she was separated
from her parents in the first years of the Revolution:[1]

'*Nyanya's* religion was rather on the negative side,
and she was frightened of the devil. The devil is part of
the folklore—something like a household god, an evil
spirit. She expected to be punished at any time, at any
minute. You must be extremely careful not to provoke
the evil spirit. Every time you do something wrong you
get punished immediately because there was something
waiting for you to do it. I was a very obedient child but
when I did do something wrong and then later bumped
myself or hurt myself, it was the punishment. So you see
it was all very convincing. . . .

'The devil gets in through your mouth. He gets into
a general location [saying this she made circular movements round her chest]. That was part of the threat.
[Makes sign of the cross over her mouth.] That was
why you made the sign of the cross over your mouth,
like this, to keep him out. The devil provokes you to be
bad and if you are sufficiently bad he can get into you
and then you are possessed. My nurse was in constant
fear of being possessed and she made me feel that.'

Later in the same interview, when this girl was talking
about her life as a Komsomol in Moscow in the late
twenties she said: 'To be appointed [to an official position in the Komsomols] to the task was a great honour.
The more you did, the more honourable your position
was. We were considering the welfare of all humanity,
not only of the Russian people. You felt the fate of the
whole world depended on you.'

[1] This informant has already been quoted on pp. 109–10.

4

While the Russian baby is swaddled, the only way it can always express its emotions is through its eyes, for its mouth may be stopped by the *nib*. It is only with its eyes too that it can explore the outside world; speaking metaphorically, one might say that Russian babies grasp or touch with their eyes. The very great importance of the eyes is maintained in adult life; all non-Russians tend to notice the great expressiveness of Russian eyes, and it is perhaps significant that the song which is often considered to be most 'typically Russian' is entitled 'Dark Eyes' ('*Ochi Chornie*').

Those Russians who believe in the soul nearly all consider that it is located somewhere inside the thorax and is expressed through the eyes; one analytically minded woman said the soul 'must be partly in the brain, because the brain is connected with the eyes and the eyes show the soul'.

Great Russians feel that they can communicate love and hate, passion and disapproval through the eyes. In folklore and fairy stories it is common for the hero and heroine to have fallen mutually in love before they have addressed a word to one another; they look into one another's eyes in the church or some other place where they can see but not speak. In the words of the proverb: 'Love finds its beginning in the eyes.' The ideal Soviet school-teacher can enforce discipline with his eyes: 'Fortunate is the teacher who is able to influence the pupil by silent reproof, by reproof of a glance or a hint.

Thanks to such ability discipline is quickly restored without waste of words or time.'[1]

5

The inhibition of exploration of the surrounding world during the swaddling period would seem to be one way in which the lack of sharp distinctions between other people in the environment, and (on an unconscious level) the distinction between the self and the not-self is perpetuated. This tendency is probably reinforced by the fear of separateness arising from the feeling of isolation and helplessness in infantile depressions.

This concept is one of the most difficult to convey, for English possesses neither the language nor (save exceptionally) the experience which the language designates. A few illustrations may possibly make the idea clearer.

The central sacrament of Western Christianity is Communion, the intimate connexion between the individual worshipper and Jesus Christ; in the Orthodox Church the central experience is *sobornost*, the Pentecostal descent of the Holy Ghost on the whole congregation simultaneously. Whereas a solitary Western communicant loses nothing by his solitude, an Orthodox believer cannot participate in *sobornost* without the presence of his fellows and peers.

In one type of old Russian *mir*, the village collective, all decisions had to be unanimous:

[1] Yesipov and Goncharov, *op. cit.*, p. 118.

'The decisions of the *mir* are achieved by unanimous agreement of all the members. If at the time of the meeting there are a few who are opposed, the meeting is considered incomplete and a failure. Peasants do not understand decisions by majority vote. They know in each case there can only be one proper decision and it should belong to the most clever and truthful of all. To find the truth, all members are supposed to join, and if the solution is found all the members have to comply with it. As a consequence, a member who is in disagreement with the general consent has only one outlet—to separate from the *mir*, which means that he will not be a member of the village any more.'[1]

The proverbs which play such an important role in Russian peasant thought emphasize the same point: 'The *mir* is like a wave; one man's thought is everybody's thought.' 'The *mir*'s conclusion is God's decision.' '*Mir* is a great man.' 'The voice of the *mir* is the voice of God.'

This stress on unanimity and the merging of individual differences is so well known in contemporary Russian life that it does not need illustrating; the young Komsomol whom I quoted earlier said, 'I say "my generation" all the time and not "I" because we never thought of ourselves individually, but always as a whole group'.

This feeling of being merged into a larger group undoubtedly gains strength from the fact that most Great Russian children are brought up in the emotional and psychological equivalent of a very large family—all the

[1] N. P. Semenov, *The Liberation of the Peasantry in the Reign of the Emperor Alexander III* (St. Petersburg, 1894).

members of a village or courtyard, uncles and aunts and cousins who all stand in nearly the same relation to the growing child as true brothers and sisters, mothers and fathers. This probably helps account for the fact that most Russians accept as a natural unit in which to live and work very large groups, by Occidental standards. In the same way a constant feature of their great plays and novels is an extremely large cast of characters compared with their Western equivalents. Judging by their literary productions, one could say that the Russian imagination (or unconscious) is very densely populated, and often by not very sharply differentiated figures. I do not think it is merely the unfamiliar names which make it so difficult for most non-Russian readers to identify all the characters in the larger novels.

Once a child is finally weaned, it does not seem as though its relationship to its own parents (at least among the lower castes) differs much in kind (though it naturally does so in degree) from its relationship with other older people. To all such people the child is meant to show gratitude, respect, and obedience. Parents do not normally impose unexplained decisions on their growing children; the Russian father is generally pictured as a succouring and protective, rather than stern and frightening, figure. The relationship between parents and older children generally approximates to a mutually respectful equality. Even in early childhood the chief disciplinarian is likely to be the moody old *babushka* or *nyanya*, a generation older than the parents, in the decline of life, and not a model which the growing child would be likely to take for his or her own development.

This does not mean that the parents and the other adults of the parents' generation do not punish or scold the child; but the punishments they inflict, though severe, are likely to be capricious, because the child has done something to annoy them, not on account of his breaking some rule.

Comparative research from a number of contrasting societies appears to demonstrate unequivocally that the development of a strict conscience, so that people will behave according to ethical imperatives (or feel guilt if they do not do so), is dependent on the parents rewarding and punishing their children, giving or withholding their love, on the basis of conformity to consistent principles that the child can understand. Without such consistency the child cannot judge how the parents would view a given act when they are not present, and so cannot incorporate the parents' approval or disapproval. In other words, he will not develop a strong ethical conscience; without such incorporated rules he cannot feel the type of guilt which produces internal discomfort for specific transgressions of specific rules.

Guilt is only one of the devices which human societies have developed for controlling their members; other devices include fear of direct reprisal; shame (the fear of disapproval from the community, or some portion of it); and pride (hope for approval of the community, or some portion of it). Most societies place their chief reliance on one of these devices; but it is unusual not to find at least traces of the other mechanisms.

The evidence suggests that Great Russians rely heavily on public shaming for social control: the *mir* controlled its members by this device;[1] more recent developments can be seen in the communist party's public purgings and 'self-criticism', and the holding up of individuals to public obloquy in the press and in factory newspapers.

The very unusual aspect of Great Russian character would appear to be the fact that this control by external shame is superimposed on more archaic diffuse guilt; the Great Russians neither possess the internalized ethical control which guides the conduct of most Occidentals,[2] nor the relative freedom from unpleasant autonomous internal emotions which seems to be characteristic of these non-European societies which place their chief emphasis on shame, such as the Trobrianders, the Lepchas, and probably the Chinese. Great Russians manifest considerable interest in large ethical problems, but are apparently little occupied with moral rules of conduct.

6

Constriction would appear to be the only consistently painful experience of infancy and early childhood that Great Russians undergo. They are fed bountifully and regularly, they are fully protected (perhaps over-protected) from cold, and no disciplines beyond their physical capacity are demanded of them. Following this physiologically contented childhood it would appear understandable that little evidence can be found in adult life of anxiety about the attainability of physical

[1] See p. 55, 'The Apology'. [2] See also below, p. 147.

gratifications; and it seems that they can postpone eating, drinking, rest (which is conceived as a positive pleasure), and other similar physical pleasures with ease and without psychological disturbance. Even under conditions of very great deprivation, most Russians maintain their optimistic belief that 'things cannot get worse, so they are bound to get better'.

What Russians value are not minimum gratifications —enough to get along with—but maximum total gratifications—orgiastic feasts, prolonged drinking bouts, high frequency of copulation, and so on. Nearly all Russians would seem to prefer a huge feast, followed by months of meagre fare, rather than a little improvement in their daily diet. These preferences were institutionalized in the religious observances of peasant Russia: the prolonged ritual fasts and the Gargantuan feasts with which Christmas and especially Easter were celebrated.

I think it is legitimate to trace a connexion between the total pleasure of the orgiastic feast, &c., and the total pleasure which the infant can be supposed to feel when it is unswaddled, nursed, and loved. Such gratifications are not merely pleasurable in themselves; they are patent and concrete reassurances that the projected rages and feared retaliation are not real, that the complete abandonment feared in depression has not taken place; total gratification—the orgy—provides an absolution for the diffuse guilt.

It seems probable that an unconscious search for such absolution underlay the prolonged drinking bouts which have been a feature of much peasant and working-class life (and also of the former merchants). Such drinking bouts were, it appears, periodic, lasted for several days at a time, and typically ended up with the destruction of much property; in the upper-caste drinking bouts a regular feature was the smashing of the mirrors in the restaurant.[1]

A very alert observer, Mrs. Oriana Atkinson, who spent several months in Moscow with her husband in 1946, relates the following suggestive anecdote about Russian drinking:

'The Russians have a story that they tell on themselves that really needs a Russian to tell it, but it goes like this. It is on the three stages of Russian drunkenness. (1) The Russian leans his head on one hand, his elbow on the table, holding his vodka glass in the other hand. He has been drinking but he is not drunk. He looks at his friend and he says, with deep sincerity, "You are my friend. You are the best friend that I have. I love you and trust you with all my heart. Yes, you are my best friend." And they have a couple of drinks on this. (2) Then the Russian continues, still leaning his head on his hand, his elbow on the table: "True, you are my best friend and I love you deeply. Although it is well known that you are a rascal, still I love you. I do not trust you, you and your sneaky friends. Everybody knows what a dastard you are, but I love you. Yes, I love you anyhow"; and they have a half-dozen drinks on that. (3) Then the speaker continues, his head still leaning on his

[1] A possible explanation of this smashing of mirrors might be that it represents a safe method of turning aggression against the self. As ego control becomes diminished under the influence of alcohol there might arise some sort of realization that the hostile and destructive wishes emanated from the self, and not from the others on whom they were projected. By destroying the mirror, which reflects the self, it may appear that the evil self is destroyed.

hand, a little more heavily now: "My best friend!" he cries in scorn. "A fine friend you are! I am surrounded by enemies! Every man's hand is against me! Why do I not die?" And his head slips off his hand, his elbow slips off the table, he slips off his chair and falls on the floor. His friend regards him silently for a moment, and then carefully lies down beside him. They sleep.'[1]

7

Psychoanalysts have found that some people are 'compulsive' in respect to a group of character traits which are often linked together (though in varying force)—the traits of neatness, orderliness, economy, punctuality, cleanliness, and the like; when such people have been psychoanalysed it has been found that a quite consistent aspect of their childhood experiences has been early and severe cleanliness training. By the standards common in the Occident the mass of Great Russians pay too little attention to these 'compulsive' traits; usual complaints of people who have to work with them is that they are chronically unpunctual, wasteful, careless, and so on.

This is one of the aspects where the contrast between the Soviet élites and the mass of the population is most marked; the Soviet leaders consider these traits of great social value and demand them from and, within the limits of possibility, impose them on the rest of the

[1] Oriana Atkinson, *Over at Uncle Joe's* (New York, Bobbs-Merrill Co., 1947), p. 36.

population. There is no evidence to show whether a conscious connexion is established between the high social value accorded to these traits and the Soviet demand that cleanliness training be started early (one of the recent child-rearing manuals demands that it should be imposed from the age of three months) and the imposition of such early discipline in the state-controlled clinics and crèches.

8

We have practically no direct evidence concerning the vicissitudes of sexual life in childhood; but all the evidence from adult life suggests that this is not an area of psychological stress. Among the lower castes potency seems to be taken for granted, and there is little evidence to suggest that sex identification is a problem or that there are fears of an individual derogating from his or her sex. Outside the directly sexual sphere the physical differences between men and women are very little stressed; it could almost be said that the difference is restricted to the presence or absence of a phallus. In the case of necessity, Russian fathers appear capable of taking over all maternal activities other than actual suckling; in general the Russian father is far more 'maternal' in his treatment of his young children than the fathers of the other societies of north-western Europe.

Because of the certainty of sex identification, and the apparent lack of psychological involvement, Russians of the lower castes do not appear to develop strong psychological defences against homosexuality; in situations where they are separated from women for considerable periods they will indulge in homosexual practices with ease, and without apparent guilt.[1] In ordinary life tenderness between men is given free verbal and physical expression.

It is perhaps worth noting that the last two paragraphs do not apply to members of the former upper castes (nor, it would seem, to many of the intelligentsia). Possibly because they were chiefly brought up by governesses and tutors belonging to different cultures and with different standards, people of these castes tended to treat sex with deep affect and considerable ambivalence; neurotic disturbances and true inversion occurred and some parents seem to have been conscious of this risk. Havelock Ellis, quoting Tarnovski, says that, at the end of the nineteenth century, the lower castes referred to homosexual practices as 'noblemen's games'.[2]

Among the upper castes there was a fairly widespread belief in what might be called patrilineal and matrilineal characteristics. Women tended to describe their husbands and all their husbands' families as gross, inconsiderate, lustful, and coarse, and to describe themselves and all their own families as fine, delicate, sensitive, and spiritual. It should be noted that this is not identical with the ascription of certain qualities to all the members

[1] This fact is regularly noted in the many books (especially French) dealing with prisoner-of-war and concentration camps of mixed nationalities in Germany during the last war.

[2] H. Ellis, *Psychology of Sex* (London, John Lane, 1936).

of one sex, such as is usual in the Occident; a man who will be seen by one woman as a delicate and sensitive brother, will be described by his wife as a coarse, inconsiderate, and sensual husband. When these characteristics were recognized, mothers, it would appear, were pleased when they could discover the 'matrilineal' characteristics in their sons, fathers when they could discover the 'patrilineal' characteristics in their daughters; mothers were pleased if their sons were spiritual, fathers if their daughters were sensual.

Together with this emotional complex of attitudes about sex there was generally very considerable verbal prudery in the upper castes and some of the intelligentsia; compared with their Continental contemporaries most Russian plays and novels are notably reticent, and even prudish. In some portions of the upper castes post-marital love-affairs were apparently frequent and passionate, becoming for some groups the chief occupation of adult life.

In the earlier years of the Soviet régime members of the communist party were required to be very abstemious in all physical indulgences; subsequently the laws and regulations were modified.

9

Although Great Russians can enjoy physical pleasures with great gusto and without apparent guilt, it seems as though they felt that nothing which happens to or with their bodies is of really major importance. The stoicism and endurance of the Russian peasant and Russian soldier have been often described, and often admired. John Rickman recalls that when he was doing medical work as a country doctor boys and girls, men and women would have two or even three teeth pulled out in a single session without any anaesthetic, and without showing a quiver of fear.

It seems comprehensible that people who pay so little attention to their own physical sufferings should also ignore those of others; and I think it probable that a good deal of behaviour which, if performed by Occidentals, would be deliberate cruelty, should rather be described as indifference when performed by Russians.

The vicissitudes of the body are of relatively little importance; the vicissitudes of the soul and of the emotions, on the other hand, are of overwhelming interest and importance. While swaddled, the Russian child has no control over his body; he can do nothing but endure the pains of constriction; all his attention is inevitably concentrated on his emotions.

At least until recent years, one of the greatest and most consistent pleasures that Russians enjoyed was giving verbal expression to the emotions momentarily possessing them, by talking in the presence of a 'sympathetic' listener. The presence of a 'sympathetic' listener is essential for the pleasure to be felt at its fullest; and by 'sympathetic' Russians do not seem to mean a person feeling the same or similar emotions, but a person who listens with feeling and understanding and without condemnation. Many Russians deny the possibility of non-Russians being 'sympathetic'. There are a number of expressions to denote this communication of emotion; one of the most common is 'pouring out the soul' (*izlivat dushu*). The ideal situation of love or friendship is when two souls are poured out together so that they mingle—in some ways a worldly analogue of the Pentecostal *sobornost*.

Although a 'sympathetic' listener is ideal, any listener at all is better than none. The person to whom no one will listen is a constantly recurring pathetic figure in the works of Chekhov and other Russian writers; and the most consistent complaints from Russians who have left Russia since the beginning of the purge trials is that one can no longer say what one feels. This privation seems to bulk very much larger than the merely physical privations, which many Occidentals would find unbearable.

Of course, the desire to have a listener when one wants to talk is universal, but the psychological urgency with which Russians desire to express their emotions to another appears unusual and specific. It seems plausible that this urgency derives from the psychological defences against the infantile depressions, with their intolerable feelings of numb loneliness; the presence of others is a patent sign that one has not been abandoned. In John Rickman's telling phrase, it is an 'unswaddling of the soul'. It is probably the same defences which make the cultivation and exploration of emotions, which most non-Russians would regard as painful, relatively pleasurable and rewarding to Russians: feeling, any feeling at all, becomes valuable in contrast to the agonized apathy of depression.

Nearly the whole of Russian literature bears witness to the intensity and zest with which Russians probe their thoughts and feelings; the common Anglo-Saxon parody of Russian plays stresses this point almost exclusively. The sitting-rooms of many Great Russians outside Russia which I have seen seem as though they were chiefly arranged to facilitate the pouring out of the soul: chairs grouped round small tables (for tea and vodka) with bright and usually unshaded lights immediately above them, so that nothing shall impede the flow of soul through the eyes.

Common Russian speech has a large vocabulary to describe emotions of varying degrees of intensity; and most Russians are articulate concerning the techniques by which unpleasant feelings can be removed or alleviated. The list which follows is illustrative, rather than exhaustive.

(i) Except for deeply religious people, and possibly the intelligentsia, the least important of the unpleasant states Russians recognize is the reproach of conscience (*soviest*). Although this term is used for the religious concept of the 'internal voice', in common speech it generally refers to minor transgressions of politeness or etiquette. This depreciation of the concept of 'conscience' is congruent with the hypothesis of the low potential of internalized ethical parental figures. For the laity faults of conscience can be removed by formal apologies which need not be sincere.

(ii) An infraction of the law or of social usage is termed *vina*. This is absolved by the appropriate punishment, without any necessary emotional change on the part of the transgressor. In this it is distinguished from

(III) a sense of sin (*grekh*) which can only be removed when the sinner has reached a state of highly emotional repentance and is then given absolution by the priest or other appropriate figure. In the case of sin the absolver's emotions are not taken into account.

(IV) To get rid of a sense of shame (*stid*) however, it is essential to induce the appropriate emotions of understanding and 'sympathy' in the person or persons wronged before they can absolve you; this is usually produced by long demonstrations of the 'sincerity' of the transgressor's repentance. The 'sincerity' refers to the strength and unambiguity of the transgressor's emotions, and not necessarily to the truthfulness of his explanations.[1]

The states so far discussed arise from actions, whether intentional or not, on the part of the sufferer; those that follow are either seen as spontaneous or as due to the behaviour of others.

(V) *Stradanyie* can probably be best translated as 'mental suffering'. It is the emotion felt for unrequited love, for the unfaithfulness or coarseness or lack of understanding of lover or spouse, and similar situations. It can be removed by a change in the emotions which gave importance to the person provoking *stradanyie*.

(VI) *Skuka* corresponds in some ways to boredom, ennui, the 'spleen' of Baudelaire and his contemporaries, a feeling of loneliness and uselessness, perhaps an attenuated version of depression. *Skuka* descends on the

[1] 'The Apology', p. 55, seems to illustrate this situation very concretely.

sufferer autonomously, without being provoked by any conscious action; if he can change his situation and start 'driving on' again, *skuka* may disappear.

(VII) There does not seem to be a single English word to correspond to the feelings described by *toska*, though the Latin word *desiderium* carries many of the same meanings. O'Brien's dictionary gives 'anguish, affliction, pain, grief; weariness, boredom, oppression, homesickness', and as an adjective or verb 'afflicted, grieved, anxious, melancholy, sad, to pine away, to long for'. The feeling of yearning for the unattainable is probably the most common aspect. *Toska* descends on a person autonomously, and there is nothing that the sufferer can do, except wait for it to pass away.[1]

(VIII) Finally, there is the concept of *pozor*, disgrace. This is really in a rather different category; it is the feeling of shame and humiliation resulting from the behaviour of other people whom one feels to be akin with oneself. It is indelible unless, or until, the situation is reversed. On the personal level it is produced by the dishonourable conduct of a person near and dear to one —a brother embezzling, a sister (in the upper castes) having an illegitimate child. This emotion can also be felt on a national scale; Stalin's speech on the defeat of Japan in 1945, when he recalled what 'we of the older generation' had felt after the Russo-Japanese war, illustrates the final wiping out of national *pozor*. Before the Revolution the feeling of *pozor* was not much cultivated or dwelt on; it is an emotion to which the communists

[1] Many of Chekhov's characters illustrate *toska*; the *Three Sisters* is perhaps particularly clear.

have publicly appealed a great deal; and they have probably lessened its impact by too frequent recourse to it. The communists have also greatly extended the pre-revolutionary use of the emotion of shame, *stid*, and appear to consider this emotion of great social value.

Before the Revolution, schools for the upper castes gave what amounted to lessons in the cultivation and expression of the emotions, by laying great stress on the evocation of the appropriate moods in the pupils when they were confronted with different works of art, above all literature. The enjoyment of such expression was not, however, confined to the upper castes; peasants had little else to do during the enforced idleness of the long Russian winter.

The Soviet élites have always been most deeply opposed to this proclivity of the mass of the Russians, and have done everything possible by education and edict to force its abandonment. Their objections seem to be founded on two arguments. It is absolutely bad for a communist to allow his will to be subordinated to his emotions, such as occurs when the soul is filled with suffering or ennui; and it is socially undesirable that attention and emotion should be directed inwards, on the feelings which cannot be modified, instead of outwards, on the material objects of the environment, when thought can be the prelude of purposeful action. Although this training and propaganda has probably been successful among the more disciplined élites, there is good reason for doubting whether the behaviour has been abandoned by the mass of Great Russians, although some of the vocabulary may no longer be generally current.

10

A trait of Great Russian character which has been frequently commented on by Russians and non-Russians alike are the sudden switches and alternations from one type of behaviour to another in complete contrast to the first. One of the great Russian character actors illustrated this trait with great vividness:

'In Russian nature there's only the breadth of a split hair between cruel, coarse, abject brutality and the greatest warmth and tenderness. The peasants will curse the Virgin Mary and a moment later kiss the hem of her dress. In the Civil War, which was in many ways more cruel than the war of the Vendée—and that was on both sides—a friend told me about a Red Company in South Russia which was cleaning up the area, one of the most cruel and pitiless groups in the whole Red Army. Well, one day this group came to a burnt-out village, without a living soul, and suddenly they heard a baby crying; they looked and found a baby just a few weeks old, alive, lying beside the corpse of his mother. Well, half-drunk and dirty bandits though they were, they took the baby and then they asked, "Who will nurse the baby?" So they invaded the next village and took a woman with a baby of the same age and killed her husband and said to her, "Citizen, you must serve the Revolution". They dragged this woman round with them several weeks, and made her nurse her own baby and the baby of the company. They took a pair of scales and used to weigh both babies on the balance every day to make certain she was feeding the company baby properly. If the company baby weighed less than hers did, they used to beat her for cheating; but during the fighting they would all protect this woman and her two babies and keep them in the rear. When they finally returned to Moscow they gave the woman one of the highest awards and made her chief nurse in an institution for orphans. . . . This is just one example of the mixture of brutality and cruelty, and sympathy and warmth. In the midst of battle they were more engaged in protecting the babies than their own selves.'

A young girl who was in Danzig when it was conquered by the Russians gave a number of other examples. The soldiers would 'go and steal anything which was left in one house and then go to the next house and give everything to the children there, beaming as if they'd given the most wonderful presents'. After they'd raped girls, 'they'd often pat them gently on the shoulders and talk consolingly to them, as if to say "Now you've done your duty"'. She told of letters she had received from girl-friends who had returned from forced work in Russia: 'They [the girls] were made to do very hard work in enormous heat with nothing to eat or drink except one tin of watery soup until they broke down. But if they broke down or got ill they were taken to a hospital and treated with the greatest care and given every possible luxury—lots of cream and cakes and everything like that. But the second they were fit to work, they were turned out again and put back on the starvation régime.'

These switches from kindness to cruelty, from brutality to gentleness could be endlessly illustrated. They are very disconcerting to most non-Russians. There is a frequently repeated prototype to this dramatic and sudden change of feeling in the infantile experience of most Great Russians. At one moment they are lonely, filled with rage, constricted by the swaddling; the next moment their limbs are free, they are held in warm and strong arms and given the bountiful breast. Then this freedom and bliss in its turn comes to an end; the babies are wrapped up as though they were unfeeling parcels and left alone with their emotions.

CHAPTER III

THE ENEMY AND HATE

I

I F T H E arguments advanced in the last chapter are correct, it will follow that the majority of Great Russians have a diffuse feeling of guilt, which is largely or entirely unconscious, and a diffuse feeling of fear, derived from the projection of their infantile hostility. This fear would appear to take the form of an emotional conviction that there exists in the external world an enemy (or enemies) who plan to constrict and destroy them, but no sort of certainty concerning the identity of the enemy.

The theory and practice of the Orthodox Church took these feelings into consistent account, and gave relief to them; the malicious enemy was identified as the devil and his minions, and minute ritual instructions were given for warding him off; the pervading sense of guilt could be at least temporarily assuaged by a full confession (or, more properly, admission of guilt) followed by ritual absolution. The practices of the Orthodox Church fulfilled a most important function in Russian society by making tolerable the greatest psychological stresses; as is common with such institutions, it also maintained these stresses and induced them (though perhaps to a somewhat attenuated degree) in those whose individual experiences or constitution differed from the norm.

Russians who believed in and practised Orthodox Christianity received enormous psychological alleviation from the absolution which followed confession; they felt freed from their guilt, and could believe that other sinners who confessed and contritely asked forgiveness could also be freed from guilt. In every Orthodox household, before the Easter confession, each member would solemnly ask the forgiveness of every other member, irrespective of age or status.

When, however, Great Russians ceased to practise Orthodox Christianity they had no technique left (with the possible exception of the orgy) for ridding themselves even temporarily of the oppression of unconscious guilt; and consequently they could not admit that others could be absolved, however completely they confessed and repented. If one's own guilt cannot be alleviated, then an enemy who has been identified appears to be irremediably wicked, and almost without human qualities, as though he were an incarnation of the scriptural devil no longer consciously believed in. As an exceptionally high-minded and religious noblewoman said of her school-teachers, 'We thought of many of our teachers as enemies, and because they were our enemies all sorts of things were allowed. If you are my enemy I can cheat you and lie to you.' When the most high-principled persons could hold such attitudes towards people they had decided were their enemies without conscious guilt, it is understandable that atheists should deny almost all human qualities to enemies who are 'unmasked'. Only complete abjection, followed by prolonged and rigorous 're-education', can permit such near-devils to go on living.

2

The Russian language is a very rich one on nearly every level; and it therefore seems significant that there are very few common-speech terms (as opposed to literary words) to identify the enemy. Perhaps the most usual phrase is *tyomniye sili*—dark or sinister forces.[1] This term is completely vague; the dark forces might be anywhere and anyone, inside or outside the individual, the group, the country. All that can be certainly known about these dark forces is their plan (conspiracy, intention) to constrain and destroy.

The most straightforward identification of dark forces in the real (as contrasted with the supernatural) world is the contemporary secular authority or forces responsible for existing constraints. Russian history, up till recent years, contains a considerable number of conspiracies to assassinate and actual assassination of figures of authority. Perhaps even more revealing is the fact that Russians in positions of authority seem to expect those

[1] *Tyomniye* means in the first place dark, but by implication sinister, suspicious, evil. To a certain extent the antonym is *krasniye*, which means in the first place red, but by implication beautiful and bright. In Russian the terms 'Red Army', 'Red Square', and so on, have also the overtone of beauty, brightness, the opposite of dark and sinister.

they control to attempt assassination and take very elaborate precautions to ward off this eventuality.

If it is believed that authority is evil, suspicious, and pervasive, attempts to overthrow it must be masked with very elaborate techniques of conspiracy. These techniques are gradually becoming known to the non-Russian world through the imitative practices of contemporary communist parties. Besides secretiveness and dissimulation, they include the testing of aspirant members by ordeal instead of by investigation, public and covert authorities, and the use of *agents provocateurs*. These techniques of conspiracy seem to be Russian rather than specifically communist. To illustrate this assumption I propose to give a long excerpt from an interview with a man who was a member of the Social Revolutionary party[1] when he was a student at Kazan University and the Moscow Institute during the first decade of this century. My informant was a younger son of a 'white' priest.

'My father's brother belonged to the People's Will party and spent many years in prison, but father was friendly with him and showed no animosity when he was free. The People's Will party was the mother of the S.R. party. . . . For me and my older brother it was as though my uncle were a founder of the S.R. party so it was natural for me to join that in our Réal school. Despite many friends among the Marxists, I never thought I could become one and I never was. I read Marx but he didn't impress me. The road I followed was a very natural one. It began in Réal school with schoolboys

[1] The programme of the S.R. stressed agrarian reform, and distrusted the urban workers.

being organized into small groups to combat the régime. Generally they were cultural groups, but all were filled with politicians. . . .

'It's difficult to tell the principle of selection. The life of a revolutionist was very short. . . . If a group of eight or ten, say, were organized, after a couple of years some of these would have run away or been arrested. And then you've got a smaller group, and then you take in new recruits and the older ones inevitably become kind of leaders. The police used to plant agents everywhere, not as leaders, and then they would arrest most of the leaders and the police agent would become more important to the new people as an old revolutionary. And by such tricks they promoted their agents. And that applied to all close revolutionary movements. With general student organizations, they were about 10 per cent. legal and 90 per cent. illegal. Usually the leaders would come from the secret party groups. It was impossible to build leadership up in any normal way. Membership in small revolutionary groups was more important than position in bigger public groups. . . .'

Q. 'How did that work?'

A. 'For example in Kazan University there were about 5,000 people in some of the big student organizations, and then there were the small secret organizations. . . . If there was a general meeting of, say, one or two thousand people, the revolutionary organization would present its most eloquent people—not usually a regular member of the organization for fear of the police. If you found a person who was ready to promote the ideas which the party believed in, he would be authorized to become the public speaker. . . . He had influence on the public but not on party members. . . .'

Q. 'Exactly how did you become a member of the S.R.?'

A. 'My older brother was a member. He never told

me but I felt it and knew it when I was thirteen or fourteen. Then I became a member of a group which listened to lectures on economics—the lecturer was an S.R. man who was supposed to be very dangerous and very revolutionary. We met secretly in one another's apartments, and then later on he—no, it was somebody else— showed me secret leaflets, very badly mimeographed, and I began to read those. Next somebody gave me a secret mimeographed book to read. It was a book by an American journalist, what is his name?—a man who was invited by Count Witte to inspect Siberia and see that the exiles were not badly treated, and he became converted to their views. It was a book on prison and exile —oh, yes, the author's name was George Kennan. He showed sympathy but no more. That book was terribly secret and dangerous and I was just given it to read for two or three nights. Later on I was given literature and pamphlets to disseminate to others. And little by little I was offered to become a party member after I had performed some difficult tasks. We were living in a conspiracy so the general rule was: never tell, if you had no need to tell, with whom you have connexions, or who belongs to the party. In that way the police could be isolated.'

Q. 'What sort of people were the police spies?'

A. 'I am happy to say that I only met two *agents provocateurs* and they were not my friends. . . .'

Q. 'Have you any idea how these student agents were recruited?'

A. 'Mostly by intimidation. The police would arrest a young person who was very successful and with whom everything was going all right, but who was a party member or close to the party. They would catch him with leaflets, and that would mean three years' detention in an honourable prison, and then he would inevitably be sent for three, four or five years to exile in Siberia.

Such a boy would be involved because he would be betrayed by a gendarme and then they would give him his choice. [Informant suddenly changed his voice and manner, till now rather loud and jovial, very markedly. His voice became very gentle and insinuating and almost feminine, and at the same time he seemed to hunch up his body.] "It's a pity for a boy like you to wreck your life in this way, and we could easily come to an arrangement. We don't want you to do anything bad, but tell us . . ." And so the boy became an agent and was given assignments, usually very easy ones at first, and then little by little they would spoil him. They used to go to committee meetings and then report back. Some became nihilists and would kill a gendarme to clear themselves of guilt.'

3

At about the turn of the twentieth century (if not earlier) the Russian authorities extended the employment of a technique for diverting from themselves the free-floating unfocused hostility of the mass of the population. This technique consisted in pointing out to the masses that there were other groups who were planning to oppress, constrain, and destroy them, with the implication (usually tacit) that the removal of existing authorities would lay the masses open to even greater constrictions. These malevolent dark forces can be discovered anywhere; they may be any foreign nation, Jews, Trotskyists, fascists, capitalists, and so on endlessly; they may be vague and far away, or they may be people very near to one—fellow-students, fellow-workers, managers, generals, high officials. This technique has been very highly developed in the last thirty years; and to-day one of the chief functions of authority is to 'unmask' and point out to the rest of the population who their enemies are.

If the hypothesis of free-floating unfocused hostility is correct, it would be understandable that Great Russians would be relieved, rather than disconcerted, by being informed that individuals or nations whom they had formerly considered friends were really 'masked' enemies;[1] they would also probably not be disturbed by the 'unmasking' of former allies and associates which has characterized Soviet foreign policy in recent years. From such evidence as is available, it would appear that many Russians were disconcerted on the unique occasion when the reverse situation took place (the Ribbentrop–Molotov pact) and an enemy was revealed as 'really' benevolent. At least to-day Russians do not admit of neutrality: he who is not completely for them is 'objectively' potentially hostile, however friendly his overt feelings or behaviour. Implicit in much current Soviet writing is the belief that no praise of the U.S.S.R. on the part of non-communist foreigners is sincere and spontaneous. If it is not hypocritical and intended to deceive, it has been extorted grudgingly and unwillingly. It is almost certainly significant that the only complicated psychological concept which is employed consistently by Russian Marxists is the concept of unconscious hostility.

[1] For a schematic illustration of this process, see the account of the phases of Russian drunkenness, quoted on p. 140.

4

Once an enemy has been 'unmasked' and identified, what should be done? It would appear that this is a question where the Soviet élite and the intelligentsia tend to give a different answer to Great Russians belonging to the traditional castes.

For the latter the proper response to the identification of an enemy is an attack of destructive rage, *zloba*, which may involve the exercise of violence, but which is quickly over. For the intelligentsia and the Soviet élites the proper response is hatred—persistent, conscious, cold negative feelings which should not be allowed to lapse. It is significant that the only word for hate—*nyenavist*—is a learned, literary word which apparently has little currency in ordinary speech.

It would seem as though an attack of rage had a somewhat cathartic effect (perhaps similar to the 'righteous anger' recognized by Anglo-Saxons) and is not avoided; and that violence—especially emotional violence—becomes valued *as an instrument* in liberating one temporarily from the diffuse unconscious guilt and fear and destroying the confusions produced by the dark forces. In the infantile situation postulated in the previous chapter, the infant was not overwhelmed by depression as long as he was raging and pushing against the constraints; and the depression would cease with the return of the feelings of rage.

On an unconscious, or at least on an unverbalized, level, lower-caste Russians would appear to establish some connexion between violence and sexual potency. Wife-beating would appear to be a not unusual pheno-menon in lower-caste marital life; and it would seem as though beating bore some relation to copulation, for beater and beaten alike. Numerous proverbs stress the point: 'Love your wife like your own soul, shake her like a pear tree'; 'Blows from one dear to you don't hurt for long'; 'I like him, so I beat him'.

In so far as violence is positively valued as an instrument for liberating one from the feelings of guilt and fear, it tends to be treated like directly physical pleasures in which quantity becomes of great psychological importance. It seems as though Russians felt a continuous psychological compulsion to go all the time to the limit of their strength and endurance. One can only know that one has gone to the limit of one's strength (done all that one should do) by a feeling of complete exhaustion, or by coming against an indestructible barrier and being repulsed and pushed back. This may be an analogue of the infantile situation in which depression is warded off by constant pushing against the constraining bonds of swaddling. It is probably this feeling which makes the tactical retreat so acceptable to Russians, Czarist and Soviet alike.[1]

The objection of the Soviet élite to attacks of rage

[1] It should be noted that although the notion of being pushed back, after one has exerted all one's strength, is acceptable, the notion of weakness, of not having the strength to exert, is almost intolerable. I have never interviewed willing informants from any other society who were so incapable of recalling incidents from their own childhood; it is as though all memories of the period of physical weakness were suppressed.

which are quickly over would seem to be of the same nature as their objections to the cultivation of the emotions: the feelings should be controlled by the will for useful social ends. Consequently in their view while anger is individualistic and undesirable, hatred is a valuable quality in the Soviet citizen and should be cultivated. The teaching of hatred plays a major role in the 1946 text-book for Soviet school-teachers already quoted:

'A morally educated individual, according to our understanding, is one who in his conduct subordinates his own interests to the service of his Motherland and his people. Such service presupposes wrath and hatred towards the enemies of the Motherland who imperil the battle-won rights of the people and all that has been created in the realm of material and cultural life by both the old and the younger generation.'

'The pupils of the Soviet school must realize that the feeling of Soviet patriotism is saturated with irreconcilable hatred toward the enemies of socialist society. Hatred gives birth to class revolutionary vigilance and creates a feeling of irreconcilability toward the class enemy; the weakness of such vigilance undermines the cause of the socialist revolution. It is necessary to learn, not only to hate the enemy, but also to struggle with him, in time to unmask him, and finally, if he does not surrender, to destroy him.'

'In all educational work devoted to the preparation of future citizens to defend the Motherland, it is necessary to remember that to vanquish the enemy is impossible without the most burning hatred of him. Passionate love of the Motherland breeds inevitably strong hatred of the enemy. Enslavers of people, destroyers of culture, and stranglers of liberty are hated by all to whom the freedom and independence of the Motherland are dear.'

'Stalin links the question of education in patriotism and in friendship between peoples with education in hatred toward enemies of the people and enemies of the Motherland.'[1]

I should like to draw attention to the vagueness with which the target for this cultivated hatred is described The enemy 'imperils battle-won rights', 'enslaves people, destroys culture, strangles liberty', is filled with malevolence; but, save that he does not devour the soul, what human traits does he possess? The Soviet school-child should be taught to hate; but this hatred appears to be as free-floating and unfocused as the guilt and fear which I have postulated for their earliest experiences.

[1] Yesipov and Goncharov, *op. cit.*, pp. 42, 62, 70, 146.

CHAPTER IV

THE LEADER, LOVE, AND TRUTH

I

SINCE THE later middle ages, and with a certain amount of interruption in the earlier years of the Soviet régime, political authority in Russia appears to have possessed two components: a Leader who is held to be all-wise and all-knowing, the embodiment of Truth and Foresight; and a minutely graded hierarchy of officials to carry out the wishes, plans, and revelations of the Leader and to transmit and interpret them to the mass of the population.

The emotional bonds between the Leader and the mass of the population have always been of a very different nature to the emotional bonds between the officials and the mass of the population. In the former case there is the greatest emotional closeness; in the latter very great emotional separation.

The Leader, whether Czar, Lenin or Stalin, has always been completely idealized by the mass of the population which loyally adheres to the régime; he is, in the most literal sense of the word, superhumanly perfect in knowledge, truth, and foresight. This belief is beyond the reach of conscious criticism. The girl who was in Danzig during the Russian conquest said of the Russian soldiers: 'They are terribly patriotic and worship Stalin, and when they get drunk they say this even more loudly'; other observers report similar behaviour; a 'white' priest spoke of 'The Czar who is the hand of God Himself'; and a passionate anti-communist said 'Stalin is the conscience of the Russian people, but in a very perverted way'.

This idealized Leader is an aspect of the mass of the Great Russian people, and in some fashion as it were a part of them, in so far as they accept him. This is illustrated for example by the fact that formerly peasants addressed the Czar with the familiar 'thou', instead of the honorific phrases they would use to officials; on ceremonial occasions to-day millions of marchers carrying huge pictures of Stalin march past Stalin, so that Stalin salutes himself as he marches past in millions of bodies. Similarly, Stalin joins the mass in applauding what he himself has just said. Stalin's constant use of the rhetorical device in which he both asks the questions and gives the answers may reflect the same concept.

Although the Leader is as it were a projection of the mass of the population, he is so idealized that the ordinary person cannot imagine himself thinking or feeling as the Leader would do, when he does not have the necessary information. This point can perhaps be most clearly seen by means of a contrast with the typical attitude of the Japanese (before their defeat) to their Emperor. Although the Japanese regarded their Emperor with the greatest veneration, it was always theoretically possible for a Japanese to know (as it were by introspection) what the Imperial will was, and to act accordingly. The typical excuse for political assassinations was that the persons assassinated were 'failing to carry out the will of the Emperor'; this implies that the assassin, his judges, and the public opinion to which he appealed, had means of knowing the will of the Emperor which were not dependent on the Emperor's pronouncements on the situation or person in question. On a less marked level, an English or American ship's captain, for example, can make decisions as the King's or President's representative without feeling (in many cases) the necessity for prior consultation and concrete authorization. With the mass of Great Russians this is not the case. They cannot know the Leader's will, in small things or great, until the Leader has declared it. Once the Leader has made the declaration, the Russians will dedicate all their energies, and easily their own lives, to the fulfilment of the expressed commands, wishes or plans. No ordinary considerations can stand in the way of carrying out the Leader's will; a course of action so started can only be stopped or reversed by the Leader himself making another statement of his will. The excesses and sudden reverses of Soviet domestic policy in recent years illustrate this situation clearly.

It would seem as though this very great idealization of the Leader were a psychological necessity to the mass of Great Russians. With the all-pervasive unconscious hostility and guilt engendered by their infantile experiences, their psychological well-being (perhaps on a certain level even their sanity) depends on preserving in the external world at least one figure completely uncontaminated by the all-pervading suspicion and fear, a figure which has no human frailties, which stands as a safe-guard against their own guilt and its consequences.

It has been a commonplace of psychoanalytic think-ing to trace a correspondence between the social figures of authority, and the earlier familial figures of authority in childhood, so that the king, or officer or policeman, can be viewed as a 'father-surrogate'. Despite the use of the term 'little father' to address the Czar (and, on occasion, Stalin) I do not think this is a major compo-nent in the figure of the Leader; to a great extent the Leader represents the *idealized self* rather than any figures in the child's environment. This concept is impossible to prove with the evidence now available, and difficult to substantiate; it was first suggested to me by such phrases as the one already quoted about Stalin being 'the conscience of the Russian people', and the consis-tency with which former Imperial officers spoke of the duty of the army to 'mother the Czar'. Such an idiom from martial men about their martial duties appeared very unusual. The mother is a strong, protective, and succouring figure to the young child; if the officers feel that they stand in a similar relation to the Czar, then, on an unconscious level, the Czar is a child, but a completely idealized child.

This hypothesis is not merely of theoretical impor-tance. If it is correct it would imply that it would be psychologically intolerable for Great Russians to live for any length of time without an idealized Leader, that a Leader is necessary to save them from political anarchy and personal disintegration.

2

The Leader guides and directs the mass of the population through the agency of a minutely graded hierarchy of officials who are under him and over the people. On occasion the Leader will by-pass this official hierarchy to enter into direct communication with some of the people and right wrongs perpetrated by his agents in his name (but without his knowledge); but such interventions can only be occasional and spasmodic, for otherwise he would be distracted from his most important work. As Lenin once remarked, 'You mustn't stroke anyone's head—you might get your hand bitten off'.[1] (Stroking the head is the conventional way in which a Great Russian father demonstrates his love for his child.)

During the greater part of Russian history, most of the positions in the hierarchy of authority were determined by heredity, but even then there were some (especially in the ecclesiastical hierarchy) which were achieved by personal abilities and ambition, even though the competition was generally within a restricted group. Since 1917 the great majority of positions have been achieved; in the early years of the Soviet régime heredity counted negatively, inasmuch as individuals might be disbarred from positions of authority, whatever their personal qualifications, if their parents were of a disapproved social class; there are some slight signs to-day

[1] M. Gorky, *Days with Lenin* (New York, International Publishers, 1932), p. 52.

that heredity is again being counted positively, for example the military cadet schools reserved for the sons of higher officers in the Soviet army.

There are at least two prerequisites for the achievement of positions of authority: knowledge through education (which is consequently extremely highly valued by those who seek or respect authority); and the renunciation of immediate pleasures. Among the pleasures which must always be renounced to achieve authority is the feeling of oneness with one's fellows, and the indulgence of emotions for their own sake; both must be replaced by conscious internal discipline. Other types of renunciation which have, or have had, power to give authority are the renunciation of sexuality and all worldly goods (which gave the 'black' priests their authority) and the abandonment of the exercise of free will and judgement, the ascetic life, and the shortening of life itself by overwork (which gave the members of the communist party their authority).[1] It is perhaps justifiable to suggest that the current policy of the leaders of the Soviet Union is to achieve authority for themselves and their country by the renunciation on the part of the mass of the population of all direct gratifications, and by using these renunciations to forge the weapons of conquest.

It is interesting to note that the Great Russians apparently do not hold the belief that authority is more

[1] Scattered evidence suggests that in contemporary Russia the rank-and-file members of the communist party no longer have special authority nor enjoy special respect. This may be connected with the tripling of the number of party members during the war years.

suited to people of certain character types than it is to others. Such notions as 'potential leadership', 'initiative', and so on, which bulk so large in Anglo-Saxon thinking, have no place in theirs. Education, obedience, and the will-power to renounce present pleasures should, it would seem, automatically bring with them the other necessary qualifications. In the Czarist military cadet schools 'authority among the cadets in the classes was given by marks, not by physical appearance or proficiency in drill, or marksmanship or anything like that. Of course, if a person got good marks, he should get the other qualities later, even though he might not be a good disciplinarian. . . . Prestige was given directly along intellectual lines, and then you should climb up to proficiency in the other branches.' Another informant, who was in a position to know, said that in current recruiting for membership in the communist party and some of its branches 'the first quality looked for is pliability, that is to say, people who will do what they are told without arguing or questioning. Too much book-reading, unless it is directly connected with professional work, is considered. an undesirable quality. So, too, is initiative, except in direct connexion with work.'

There is even some evidence to suggest that 'natural leaders' who create circles of students and so on around themselves are looked on askance; their ascendancy is likely to be due to their defiance of existing authority. Thus school-teachers are warned 'Sometimes friendship between children is formed on the basis of negative interests or even harmful mutual "enterprises". On noticing such a development the teacher should take measures . . . to destroy the friendship by dispelling the halo of the "friend-leader" . . .'[1]

As has already been said, people who become members of the hierarchy of authority abandon all feelings of identification with their fellows, and as a consequence all feelings of equality. An illustration of this can be found in the use of a pronominal adjective; ordinary non-official Great Russians habitually speak of 'our peasants'; officials speak of 'the peasants'. Somewhat similar is Stalin's instruction to teachers: 'People must be grown carefully and tenderly, just as a gardener grows a favourite fruit tree.'[2] A gardener may give his favourite fruit trees the best possible care, the most ideal treatment; but this can never imply a feeling of identity or equality between the gardener and what he cares for.

Among those in authority, the feeling of equality is replaced by the most rigid insistence on hierarchy and one's relative position in it; members of the governing élite show the greatest intellectual contempt for the concept of *uravnilovka*—egalitarianism, the attempt to make equal those who are naturally unequal. It seems probable that one reason why communists are so much more hostile towards and contemptuous of social democrats (Labour) than of more right-wing parties abroad is because of their adherence to this despised doctrine.

The preoccupation with relative status in the Russian official hierarchy would seem to be a major source of the 'bureaucratic spirit' which is so constantly inveighed against and satirized in Czarist and Soviet speeches, books and periodicals.

[1] Yesipov and Goncharov, *op. cit.*, p. 61.   [2] *Ibid.* p. 38.

3

The relationship between the élite in authority and the mass of the population they constrain and guide is ideally one of complete superordination and subordination, of activity on the one side and of passivity on the other.

This is the ideal, but it is only attained under certain conditions. Just as those in positions of authority abandon their feeling of 'oneness' with the mass of the people over whom they are placed in authority, so do the mass of the people apparently feel that those in authority are 'apart' from themselves. This would seem to be a derivative of the fact that the earliest constraining 'authority'—the swaddling—is not part of the self, and is not personified.

The analogy of swaddling illustrates very clearly the relations that exist between people in authority and people under authority. The qualities most demanded from authority is that it should be firm and consistent, neither too tight nor too loose, and, above all, not shifting capriciously from excessive severity to excessive lenience. There seems to be a general tendency to 'test' authority; if it is not firm and consistent, it will be first disregarded and then cast off.

For obvious reasons, it was impossible to do consistent interviewing on attitudes to accepted political authority; it was a subject fraught with too much danger in the greater number of cases. I therefore concentrated on what appeared to be the nearest 'safe' and non-political analogue to political authority, the attitude towards teachers and schoolmasters. These attitudes, both from informants brought up under the Czarist régime and from those brought up under the Soviets, fell into two sharply contrasting groups: an attitude of mutually respectful equality, indicated by the fact that teacher and pupil addressed one another in identical terms (first name and patronymic); and the treatment of the teacher as somebody alien and potentially hostile. The most eloquent illustration of this latter attitude was given by the Czarist cadet, already quoted; similar attitudes were expressed by people brought up under the Soviets, but with less clarity. He was talking about cliques among the students, and said that some of them had their chief interest in fighting authority. I asked what he meant:

A. 'It all depended on who was in authority. If it was a weak person advantage was taken of him very cruelly and unfairly. If he was strong, he was respected and liked, odd as it may seem. And if there was a strange man, life was made hell for him. He was just hounded.'

Q. 'What happened?'

A. 'Cadets used to see how far they could go. There were some specialists in the fight against authority, and the class would observe what happened to them. In my clique, we were intellectual challengers, and we would argue and resist on an intellectual plane.'

Q. 'And what would happen if it was a strong man?'

A. 'Oh, he would slap down opposition. What we liked above all was consistency. We hated people who were strong one day and weak another.'

Q. 'Was there friendship between the professors and cadets?'

A. 'No, you'd never say there was any real friendship; it was very formal.'

Q. 'And when you say you made life hell for a stranger, what does that mean?'

A. 'Oh, we'd tease him and shout and wouldn't listen to him. We'd turn our backs when he spoke. We'd put pins and thumb-tacks on his chairs, smelly nutmegs on the end of his pencil, and anything else. . . .'

Q. 'Could you tell lies to the teacher?'

A. 'Oh, sure. We all lied to our teachers. It was all right to lie to any of our superiors, but not to other students. There was a feeling that teachers were, you might say, fair game. . . . You could lie to defend yourself. A few didn't but most of them did if they were accused. There was a lot more lying than one would have thought. In Russia there was much antagonism to the teachers as such. The teachers never took the students into their confidence. You could say it was really a battle of wits against authority. No co-operation was attempted. It was a warfare.'

Thus far the Czarist pupil of more than thirty years ago. Note how closely his attitudes correspond with the instructions given to Soviet school-teachers in 1946:

'Moral demands must always be made upon schoolchildren in a decisive form and be carried into life with firm insistence. It is entirely inadmissible for a teacher at one time to punish pupils strictly for errors, and at another "not to notice".'

'Consistency must be observed by all adults who share in the rearing of the young. The several teachers of a given child should not contradict each other, but rather should follow a single line. As his teachers change, provision should be made for an orderly and consistent sequence of influences. When a child passes with age from certain teachers to others, he suffers injury if he encounters an entirely different treatment, if, for example, mildness changes sharply to severity, or if *firmness changes to weakening softness.*'

'An individual possessing volitional qualities of character is consistent; with him words do not contradict deeds and acts harmonize with convictions. Children form their convictions in school and become habituated to conscious and definite consistency in their actions. These traits of character are developed gradually and in the face of serious difficulties.'[1]

4

In all relations which are not defined as leader and led, superordinate and subordinate, Great Russians who are not in the authority hierarchy demand the most absolute equality in their personal relationships. It would appear that Russians do not conceive of any intermediate positions: there is either complete equality, or complete superordination and subordination. This may derive from the situation in which the infant experiences weakness as the absolute weakness of depression, not the relative biological weakness of being smaller. For the Great Russians, weakness, like power, is absolute.

Some examples of this demand for equality, until it almost becomes a merging of personalities, have already been given, and more could easily be found: the village *mir* and the Soviets and collectives formed on the same

---

[1] Yesipov and Goncharov, *op. cit.*, pp. 46, 49, 122. My italics.

model, the Pentecostal experience of *sobornost*. Situations which outside Russia are viewed as competitive or exhibitionist will often be rephrased by Russians as positions of symmetrical equality. Thus the great actor, already quoted, compared the relationship between actor and audience to that between tennis partners! 'I don't play *for* the audience—that is cheap and bad—but *with* the audience. There is no rivalry, no looking for effect, but pure sport. You send the ball to the audience and they send it back to you. If you lose the ball that is your fault. But if the audience misses the ball, you win. The audience misses the ball when you place it where they don't expect it and they are surprised.'

Many of the dramatic changes which have taken place in the organization of the Red Army can, I think, be traced to the fact that the Russians can envisage no alternative between the most complete superordination and stress on rank, and complete equality. An observer who saw something of the Red Guard in the early days of the Revolution wrote:

'The Bolshevik recruits were familiar with the village form of government. It was therefore natural that they should introduce into their army the same type of administration and discipline which obtains in the *mir* or village council. In our sense of the word, discipline was lax, but the spirit of brotherhood was strong, and the men were accustomed to acting upon the compelling force, not of orders from a superior officer, but of the will of the meeting. Putting this into other words, the men obeyed a committee of the regiment or platoon, which was elected by themselves and which took its authority solely from the will of the regiment or platoon expressed in mass meetings. . . . The Bolsheviks were good at guerrilla warfare.'[1]

It would seem as though the only alternative to this type of organization, which could not possibly be effective on a large scale, is a hierarchy of officers with rights and privileges far greater (relatively) than those enjoyed by officers in any Occidental army.

I think the same principle—the idea that the only alternative to complete equality is complete subordination—can be seen operating in much of the Soviet Union's foreign policy. The proposed establishment of the United Nations' police force, for example, was nullified by the Soviet's insistence that the contributions of all the great powers should be absolutely equal (so that the navy and air force could not be greater than four times China's contribution). Similarly, the dispute with Marshal Tito of Yugoslavia would seem to have as a major component the fact that, while paying the Soviet Union every respect, Tito was not willing to concede its absolute, but only its relative, superiority, that he would admit his country to be only relatively, and not absolutely, weaker. Whatever their conscious intentions may be, it would appear that the Soviet élites find it psychologically impossible to permit their satellites relative independence, because it is a state they cannot envisage. The moment the balance is tipped, to the slightest measurable degree, from complete equality, they seem to fear that they will become completely subordinate;

[1] John Rickman, *An Eye-witness from Russia* (London, People's Russian Information Bureau, 1919), reprinted from the *Manchester Guardian*.

the moment a subordinate shows the slightest independence they seem to fear that the process will not stop until the subordinate is in a position of complete equality or else completely superordinate. In the expressive metaphor of Dr. Leites, the Soviet élites have avalanche fantasies. It would seem legitimate to make a connexion, on an unconscious level, between these fantasies and the horrible experience of being overwhelmed by the impotence of depression; and also with the feeling of destructive omnipotence when the depression gives way to rage.

5

With the partial exception of the relationship between a parent and a young child, the most tender emotions which Russians express are those between complete equals. Of these the most dramatic is passionate love; but Great Russians seem to regard this emotion with some ambivalence, because it is conceived as being so completely outside individual control or the dictates of reason; in the words of the proverb, 'Love is evil; for you can even fall in love with a goat.' Overwhelming passion—*strast*—is thought likely to lead to disaster.

For many years, one of the most popular forms of amusement (especially among factory workers) has been the singing of comical or ironical quatrains called *chastushki* to the accompaniment of an accordion. Many of them are traditional; but new ones are constantly being invented to suit new circumstances. In their function—though not in their contents—they somewhat resemble the limerick. One of the most constant themes of the traditional *chastushki* (the new ones are chiefly political or technological) are the defects of the beloved.

I have a sweetheart
And it's a shame to walk with her in the streets;
All the cab drivers are angry
Because all their horses bolt when they see her.

My darling weighs seven *pood*
And she's afraid of camels.
But the camels got so scared
That they ran away from her for miles.

Behind our house
All the grass is trampled.
It's not a horse and it's not a cow;
It's all damned love.

My darling sits on the stoops
With an expression on his face.
I did not think long;
I came close and spat.

I suffered and suffered
And threw myself from the bridge into the river.
On account of you, you devil,
I swam for three hours.

On the far horizon
A cloud humped its back.
My darling girl jumped with a parachute
From behind the cloud.

I am yours and you are mine;
Do anything you want with me.
If you want, you can lose me at cards,
And if you want you can give me to your comrades.

Out of a very considerable collection of *chastushki* this last one is the only one of those dealing with love between the sexes which does not express some negative feeling about the beloved. And even in this case a number of people who were discussing it thought 'the girl wouldn't mind going to his comrades for a change'!

These *chastushki* it must be emphasized are exclusively lower-caste, and only refer (in the main) to lower-caste emotions. As far as I could discover, none are obscene; and obscenity appears to play little part in Russian humour (though a major role in Russian invective). In true literature and poetry (as opposed to folk-poetry) there are many lyrical and whole-hearted descriptions of passionate love, though even there (I have the impression) such love is likely to be tragic and disastrous.

6

The most widespread tender emotion that Great Russians value can perhaps be called sympathy-pity. English possesses no single word which covers the connotations of the Russian terms (*zhalitsia, sochustvovat', otzivchivost*), though 'pity' is the most usual translation. But the emotion described is both less and more than pity (as it is used in English or American); it is less than pity because it generally excludes the feeling for the mentally and physically handicapped, the maimed or the physically sick; it is more than pity because it is as desirable—perhaps more desirable—to be the recipient of another's sympathy-pity, than to offer this sympathy-pity to another. Mutual sympathy-pity is often the forerunner of successful and happy love. It can perhaps be defined as 'a sympathetic understanding and feeling for the moral and spiritual anguish which others are undergoing'.

This emotion can be felt for everybody undergoing moral and spiritual anguish, whether they are known and seen or not. An often-quoted poem by Alexander Blok on this emotion tells:

> A girl was singing in the church choir
> Of all the tired in foreign lands,
> Of all the ships that went to sea,
> Of all who lost their joy. . . .

It is the emotion felt for the down-trodden and oppressed, for criminals and convicts. It is above all on this emotion that the Soviet leaders play to mobilize the Great Russians to the missionary task of liberating the down-trodden and oppressed in the rest of the world.

The common use of the reflexive form (*zhalitsia*) and the connotations of the emotion suggest that, on an unconscious level, the object of pity-sympathy is felt to be similar to, or 'the same as', the person feeling the emotion. But to be a proper recipient of such an emotion the object must be already suffering mental and spiritual anguish. This has two implications: the Great Russian thinks of himself as suffering, and the suffering of the other is not the fault of the pity-sympathizer, is not produced by his acts or wishes. If the hypothesis of diffuse unconscious hostility and guilt is correct, it is understandable that there is reassurance in the certainty that one is not responsible for the other's unhappiness; and also that this emotion (unlike the passionate love portrayed in the *chastushki*) is not contaminated by negative and hostile feelings.

Similar reasons may be the cause for the fact that the same terms are not normally used for the feeling for the physically incapacitated or mutilated, the maimed, the halt, and the blind (nor for such positive feelings as exist for other people's children); the physical differences prevent the feeling that these sufferers are 'the same as' oneself, and it is possible that these gross physical misfortunes arouse too much unconscious guilt. The common terms used to describe the emotion felt for such unfortunates are comparatively lightly toned; for example, *shchadit*, to take care of, to tend.

It would seem that the feeling that the Leader and his associates have for the mass of the people is nearer to tending than to sympathy-pity. The Leader looks after the masses, but he controls his feelings for their moral and spiritual anguish; he 'grows them carefully and tenderly, like a gardener growing a favourite fruit tree'.

7

The Leader and his associates cannot indulge their feelings of sympathy-pity, just as they cannot indulge in any other emotions for their own sake; for to do so would distract them from their occupation in the most important activity of mankind—the gradual discovery and application of the Truth, *pravda*.[1] In the Russian conception of the universe, their concept of Truth holds an extremely important place.

The concept of Truth can be likened to a circle which surrounds one; it is analogous to the horizon which bounds the limitless and featureless Russian steppe. This steppe is, for very many Great Russians, the 'typical' Russian landscape, no matter what sort of country or town they may actually have been reared in; and it is often used, both by them and by non-Russians, as an illustration and explanation of Russian character. A distinguished Russian said:

'I think you can say that Russian psychology is conditioned by their geography and their history. In Russia there is no rational shelter from the ever-present threat from outside. The Russians are brave in the face of disasters they expect, but all the time they are looking round for ways of avoiding their enemies. You must keep in mind that they grow up in those enormous steppes with nothing to prevent them galloping mile after mile in any direction in a literal fashion; and figuratively you have this great width of character with no restrictions, no limits on what they think they can have. . . . Russians are rather lost in those vast spaces where they live. They have nothing to cheer them up. . . . Russians are always living on the same level, seeing everything from the same aspect. Mountaineers have songs glorifying the storms and new impressions and new thoughts, but on the plains life and the view are monotonous. There is nothing but monotony and lone-

[1] Much of this analysis of *pravda* is founded on concepts developed by Dr. Margaret Mead and Mr. N. Calas.

liness. . . . In Russia the soul plays a great part . . . there are no mountains, no sea; only agriculture, the forest, the marshes, and the endless plain, and there are long periods of winter rest which give time to consider things of immaterial interest.'

In actual material fact, the great plains of Russia are not—at least to the casual traveller—more immense or featureless than the plains of the Middle West United States, or large areas of India, China, Indo-China, or Argentina; but Great Russians (and, as already said, very many non-Russians) consider this featureless landscape relevant to the understanding of the Russian character, in a fashion quite different to the relevance commonly attributed to the other areas named in the formation of the characters of their inhabitants. Possibly a connexion can be traced between the belief in the relevance of the limitless plain bounded by the horizon and the fact that in the typical childhood experience intense feeling is diffused (not concentrated) on the periphery of the body where it is bound by the swaddling, and the interior of the body is felt to be 'featureless' without objects on which the attention can fasten.

The concept of Truth can be likened to a circle which surrounds one. Truth exists, one and indivisible, and it can be discovered and applied. There is not a 'core' or 'heart' of Truth with a series of applications which may be more or less correct. Truth is rather a system of inter-connected items, arranged in a hierarchy, but in such a way that the destruction of one item jeopardizes the whole system. There is no concept of relative truths or of the possibility of various 'aspects' or 'versions' of truth. As a consequence compromise is inadmissible (except perhaps as a tactic); and there is no possibility of a 'loyal opposition'. All men of good will must recognize the Truth when it is pointed out to them; if they refuse to recognize it, this shows their wicked characters and evil intentions. To accept the decision of the majority, without the appropriate internal convictions, is for Great Russians the abandonment of all honour and self-respect; to submit willingly to those you are convinced do not possess the Truth is an act of baseness.

Although Truth is a coherent system, it is not consistent according to the usual standards of Occidental logic. Truth embraces contradictions both in space and time; the fact that the truth revealed to-day, or the application of the truth demanded to-day, is not the same as the truth (or application) of yesterday, does not mean that one or the other ceases to be part of Truth. Truth is so great that it contains all contradictions; Russians do not reject these contradictions, nor is it certain that they perceive them as contradictions, in the way non-Russians would do.[1]

The Leader and the hierarchy of authority under him see the Truth more clearly than the led, and they impart their discoveries and applications to the latter. But all Great Russians, however ignorant and however humble,

[1] In his book *The Russian Idea* (London, Bles, 1947) the famous theologian Nicolas Berdyaev documents the manner in which Hegel's dialectic—the philosophy of contradictions—was eagerly embraced by 'us Russians' from the moment it was published. It was felt to be particularly congenial to all shades of Russian thought, both in its idealist and its materialist (Marxist) versions.

feel that they are part of the Pentecostal Congregation and have partaken of *sobornost* and so live in the Truth and follow it to the extent of their capacities. It is this conviction that they live in the Truth and pursue it as do the people of no other nation which gives the mystical overtones to the phrase 'Holy Russia' and the newer form 'Soviet Motherland'. It is this conviction which binds the Russians in the sure belief of their righteousness and superiority and gives them their seeming unyielding rigidity, whether the present aspect of the Truth be Orthodox Christianity, or the latest version of Leninism-Stalinism.[1]

[1] Note these two quotations from Berdyaev (*op. cit.*, pp. 2, 8). 'The Russians have not been in any sense a people of culture, as the peoples of Western Europe have been, they have rather been a people of revelation and inspiration.'

'In what respect was the conception of Moscow as the Third Rome twofold? The mission of Russia was to be the vehicle of the true Christianity, that is, of Orthodoxy, and the shrine in which it is treasured. This was a religious vocation. "Orthodoxy" is a definition of "the Russians". Russia is the only Orthodox realm, and as such a universal realm like the First Rome and the Second.'

CHAPTER V

CONCLUSIONS

IF THE views expressed in the previous chapters are correct, the following statements can be made about Great Russians. Most important of these perhaps is the fact that there are very marked differences in character between the Soviet élites on the one hand, and the mass of the population on the other. The mass of the population is oppressed by diffuse feelings of guilt and hostility, but shows very little anxiety. They tend to oscillate suddenly and unpredictably from one attitude to its contrary, especially from violence to gentleness, from excessive activity to passivity, from orgiastic indulgence to ascetic abstemiousness. They endure physical suffering with great stoicism and are indifferent about the physical sufferings of others. They also tend to oscillate between unconscious fears of isolation and loneliness, and an absence of feelings of individuality so that the self is, as it were, merged with its peers in a 'soul-collective'. They have deep warmth and sympathy for all whom (at a given time) they consider as 'the same as' themselves; they direct their vague and unconscious hostility on all whom they consider 'different to' themselves, paying little attention to which figure is momentarily the focus for their hostility. They seem to expect hostility from all who are 'different'. They consider themselves superior to the rest of the world, because they and their country are the special repository of the Truth, one and indivisible; it is their duty to make this Truth prevail. They have a tendency to confuse thought and action. They pay little attention to order, efficiency, and punctuality. They are much preoccupied with the exploration and verbalization of the feelings momentarily possessing them. They submit unwillingly but resignedly to firm authority imposed on them from above, and merge themselves willingly with an idealized figure or Leader.

The intelligentsia and élites seem to share the diffuse guilt and hostility and to see potential enemies all around them, including the mass of the people they control. In contrast to the mass of the population, they value and cultivate the power of the will, as opposed to the emotions; they pay great attention to order, efficiency, and punctuality. They consider that people (and peoples) are fundamentally and naturally unequal, but that equality can be precariously preserved by paying attention to every minute detail. The only alternative they conceive to this precarious equality is complete superordination or complete subordination, complete power or complete weakness; and they are haunted by fears that they will be in the position of complete subordination, complete weakness. They consider themselves to be in possession of the Truth to a greater degree than the mass of the population, and would appear to have esoteric versions of the Truth which cannot safely be communicated to outsiders.

All Great Russians seem to feel the psychological compulsion to exert their strength to the limit, and to place value on violence as a means of liberation and producing order out of confusion; but here, as in all other domains, the élites consider that both efforts and violence should be subordinate to the will, while the mass of the population consider that they should be responses to appropriate autonomous emotions.

On the basis of these generalizations, it would seem possible to derive the following political maxims:

(i) It is useless to try to make friends with, or win the sympathy of, the mass of the Great Russian people, in the hopes of producing transformations of policy. The mass of the people never have had, and (in any foreseeable future) are not likely to have any appreciable influence on the policies their leaders adopt. Policy, both foreign and domestic, is determined by a very small group.

(ii) The leaders suspect that those they lead are hostile towards them, and they seek to divert this hostility on to other figures. If the leaders were to feel convinced that the mass of the population (or a sizeable portion of it) were becoming disaffected from them and favouring some outside power, this might well exacerbate the leaders' fears and induce them to precipitate a war, as the most efficacious way of diverting hostility from themselves.

(iii) No techniques are yet available for eradicating the all-pervasive suspicion which Great Russians, leaders and led alike, feel towards the rest of the world. This suspicion springs from unconscious and therefore irrational sources and will not be calmed, more than momentarily, by rational actions.

(IV) Great Russians, leaders and led alike, will continue to go all the time to the limit of their strength. They will expand their boundaries like a flooded lake, and this flood will only be contained by the political equivalent of a firm and solid dike. To continue the analogy one step further, the Great Russians will always seek out weak places or gaps in this dike; and if they find them they will exploit them.

(V) The analogy of the dike describes the only type of political behaviour which will contain Russian expansion: firmness, strength, consistency. And the greatest of these is consistency.

(VI) It should be remembered that the strategical retreat is a highly acceptable manœuvre to Great Russians. (We have no information as to how this is viewed by the other peoples of the U.S.S.R.) To be forced back means that one has gone to the limit of one's strength and endurance, done one's utmost. It is not necessarily a humiliation.

(VII) In negotiations with Great Russians, a successful outcome is most likely if negotiations are phrased in the terms of the most concrete and symmetrical equality: man for man, ton for ton, acre for acre, town for town, and so on. In the view of Great Russians, the only alternative to the most rigorous equality is for one of the parties to be completely subordinate; and they always have the fear that they may be forced into the position of absolute weakness.

(VIII) Ideological arguments, notes of admonition

and disapproval, and the like, are a complete waste of time and energy, as far as the Great Russians are concerned. With the Great Russian concept of Truth, *pravda*, it is impossible for them to admit error in any one instance, for that would destroy their whole system of Truth, and their self-esteem. If one action or attitude is wrong (incorrect) then all are wrong; and such an admission is only forthcoming in a religious conversion or political purge trial. Neither of these is likely to happen on an international scale.

(IX) There is no likelihood of Great Russians voluntarily engaging their country in any form of international organization which might conceivably give to other countries the possibility of constraining them. Consequently, it is a waste of time to discuss, for example, the abolition of the veto in the Security Council of the United Nations. There is no possibility of the development of a 'world state', as now conceived, except under complete Russian domination, while the U.S.S.R. is an independent power with Great Russians in most of the positions of authority.

(X) Although the Russians will resist every encroachment, while themselves encroaching to the greatest possible degree, there would seem to be no necessity for war between the Western Powers and the U.S.S.R. The one situation which might evoke war (apart from the Western Powers 'compressing' Russia) would be if the Western Powers manifested such weakness, or such alternations between strength and weakness, that the Russians would feel compelled to advance to such a degree that the Western powers would feel that the menace was intolerable. If Russia is faced with *permanent* strength, firmness, and consistency there would appear to be no reason why a tolerable and durable *modus vivendi* should not be maintained indefinitely.

Appendices

APPENDIX I

DEVELOPMENT OF THE SWADDLING HYPOTHESES

BY GEOFFREY GORER

NOTE: *Although in what follows I am presenting the development of my own views, I should like the reader to be as sharply aware as I am that these ideas could never have reached this degree of clarity without the constant assistance of and exchange with my collaborators on the Columbia Research Project. These ideas could never have been developed at all without the help and knowledge of my teachers and friends in anthropology and psychology: the late Dr. Ruth Benedict, the late Professor Bronislaw Malinowski, Dr. Margaret Mead, Professor Clark L. Hull, Mr. Earl Zinn, Dr. John Rickman, Dr. Harold Lasswell. I also owe an inestimable debt to three thinkers whom I never met (and have read the works of only one of them with any consistency): I. P. Pavlov, Franz Boaz, and Sigmund Freud.*

I

AS FAR AS my reading and inquiries have gone, there is no precedent in the literature of anthropology, psychology or psychoanalysis to the hypotheses developed in the previous chapters on the derivatives of muscular restraint by swaddling. It therefore seems as though it might be of some interest to outline briefly the steps by which I was led to develop these hypotheses.[1]

I should like once again to reiterate the fact that I have undoubtedly over-emphasized the importance of swaddling because, as the following pages are intended to make clear, it was one of the chief clues which I used for interpreting Russian behaviour. For me it is a clue, not a cause, of Russian behaviour; but without this clue I do not think I could have made the deductions I have. Other workers might well have reached the same results by a different route.

I approach the attempt to describe the national character of a society without being in the territory of that society by the assumption of a highly self-conscious ignorance. This ignorance has to be much more self-conscious than in the case of field-work; in the field every sight and experience emphasizes this ignorance and also produces material to modify it; when one is relying on interviews with exiles and emigrants and symbolic material (books, pictures, films, &c.) this ignorance must be constantly kept in the forefront of the mind. By ignorance I mean that I ignore, for the time being, any ideas, impressions or prejudices I may have acquired through visits to the country in question, acquaintance with members of the society being investigated, experience or recollections of their works of art, literature, and music, reactions to newspaper reports of

[1] For a review, analysis and bibliography of the existing literature see: Phyllis Greenacre, 'Infant Reactions to Restraint' (*American Journal of Orthopsychiatry*, Vol. XIV, No. 2, April 1944).

the behaviour of that nation's government, and so on. Subsequently, I may use any or all of this material to test hypotheses developed in the course of the work; but my initial position is that I know nothing whatsoever about the society I am investigating.

Although I assume that I know nothing about the society under investigation, I assume that I know certain laws about societies in general and about human beings in general, and that my task is to discover the particular manifestations of these general laws in the present instance. Following Malinowski, though maybe with modifications, I assume that every society, from the simplest to the most complex, possesses the same basic institutions and cultural imperatives, and that these institutions are intelligible only in terms of the needs—basic and learned—that they satisfy; following what I believe to be the basic underlying assumptions of Freud and Hull, I assume that human behaviour is understandable, and is derived from the operation of the laws of learning on the innate biological drives and processes of physical maturation which are common to all human beings. When I made the initial study of national character away from that nation's territory (the study of the Japanese in 1941) I developed a set of twelve postulates; with the possible exception of postulate (VII) (the assumption that fear and anger are not innate) my subsequent experience and study have not led me to abandon them; and I will therefore repeat them here.

(I) Human behaviour is understandable: with sufficient evidence it is possible to explain any observed behaviour, however incongruous isolated items may appear.

(II) Human behaviour is predominantly learned. Although the human infant may be born with some instincts and is born with some basic biological drives whose satisfaction is necessary to its survival, it is the treatment which the infant receives from the other members of the society into which it is born, and its experiences of its environment, which through the gratification or frustration of its needs enables it to learn new needs and new methods of gratification. (In this context I should perhaps state that I assume that, in a large society, genetic peculiarities do not involve any major inherent psychological differences in comparison with other large societies.)

(III) In all societies the behaviour of the component individuals of similar age, sex, and status shows a relative uniformity in similar situations. This is equally true in unformulated and unverbalized situations.

(IV) All societies have an ideal adult character (or characters, depending on sex and status) which is of major importance for parents and other adults in authority in selecting which items of children's behaviour to reward, and which to punish.

(V) Habits are established by differential reward and punishment (indulgence and deprivation) chiefly meted out by other members of the society.

(VI) The habits established early in the life of the individual influence all subsequent learning, and therefore the experiences of childhood are of predominant importance.

(VII) The chief learning in early childhood consists of the modifications of the innate drives of hunger, thirst, optimum-temperature seeking, pain avoidance, sex and excretion, and of the (possibly secondary) drives of fear and anger (anxiety and aggression) and of the biological derivatives of maturation, which are demanded by the adult members of the society; consequently a knowledge of the types of modifications imposed, the means by which they are imposed, and the times at which they are imposed, is of major importance in the derivation of adult behaviour.

(VIII) Since, in the greatest number of societies, it is predominantly the parents who reward and punish their children, the attitudes of the child to his father and mother, and, to a lesser degree, to his brothers and sisters, will become the prototypes of his attitudes towards all subsequently met people. In societies where the disciplinary role is normally taken by adults other than the biological parents, the attitudes towards such adults also become of major importance.

(IX) Except in situations of the greatest physiological stress, adult behaviour is motivated by learned (derived, secondary) drives or wishes superimposed upon the primary biological drives.

(X) Many of these wishes are unverbalized or unconscious, since the rewards and punishments which established the habits of which these wishes are the motives were undergone in early childhood, before the acquisition of speech, or because the verbalization of these wishes was very severely punished; consequently people very often cannot express their motives in words, and the motives have to be deduced from the observation of what satisfactions are actually obtained from different courses of behaviour.

(XI) When these wishes, acquired through early learning, are shared by a majority of the population, some social institutions will eventually be developed to gratify them; and institutions which originate in other societies and are then subsequently adopted will be modified to congruence with these wishes (to the extent that this is possible without impeding the gratification of the primary drives).

(XII) In a homogeneous society the cultural patterns of superordination and subordination, of arrogance and deference, will tend to show a certain consistency in all institutions from the family to the religious and political organizations; and consequently the patterns of behaviour demanded in all these institutions will mutually re-enforce each other.[1]

A reproach to studies of this nature which is frequently voiced is that they ignore the influence of history, economics, geography, and similar 'impersonal' phenomena. To my mind, this reproach would only be justified if any claim, overt or implied, were made that studies of national character were meant to describe all the phenomena of a nation's life; as far as the studies I have made are concerned, all that is attempted is the

[1] Originally mimeographed, late 1941, in the Institute of Human Relations, Yale University; subsequently printed in the *Transactions of the New York Academy of Sciences* (Series II, Vol. 5, March 1943) and *Penguin Science News No.* 1 (London, 1945). I have made a few verbal modifications here.

isolation and description of the main motives of the majority of the population over and above those rational ones which are gratified by the operation of the institutions which historical accident and technological development have produced at a given time.

For example, marketing (the exchange of goods or services) performs similar basic functions in all societies; I try to isolate what specific functions, beyond the acquisition of articles of use, prestige or profit, marketing has for members of a given society. Anybody who has done shopping in a number of different countries will know that these are very various: in one society the pleasure may be in skill in bargaining, so that the vendor feels defrauded if his first asking price is paid without demur; in another the vendor may feel gratified if he has passed off an imperfect article at a high price, while in yet another he may get greater satisfaction from an experienced and discriminating buyer who manifests his appreciation and knowledge of the vendor's skill and taste; and so on, with a very great number of variations and permutations. I consider it my business to isolate this psychological 'surplus value' and to attempt to bring it into relationship with other similar manifestations; the description of the operation of the market as an economic institution I leave to the specialists in such matters. If it is necessary to the development of my argument I may quote from some recognized authority on the subject; but I have not the training to conduct independent research; and I assume that the recognized authorities are as available to interested readers as they are to me.

The case of history is parallel. I do not question for a

moment the importance of historical developments, but the study of these is not my speciality. I am interested in how members of a society *interpret* their own history, and in some cases have made great use of this;[1] but I have nothing original to contribute to history as such. In the course of this Russian study I have read more than half a dozen Histories of Russia for my own instruction; but this is reflected in only two or three phrases in the text.

The history of religion and theology will tell how and when Roman Catholicism, for example, was adopted in different countries, and the formulation of its dogmas: I want to understand why, in the religious pictures and statues of one country, great emphasis is placed on Jesus as an infant or child, and the Virgin Mary as a young girl; in another on Jesus as a mature and bearded man, and Mary as a mature and maternal woman; in a third on Jesus as tortured and crucified, Mary as an older and grieving woman. All these figures are contained in Roman Catholicism; my interest is to discover what psychological mechanisms have influenced the choice in any given case.[2]

[1] In the case of the Russians, I think the century-old complaint that other countries are keeping them from a 'warm-water port' probably has important psychological implications; but I have not, so far, been able to discover what these are.

[2] I have not made any exhaustive study of Russian iconography; but my impressions of what I have seen are that there is an almost complete absence of representations of Jesus as a child or adolescent, or of Mary as a young girl. (The usual method of referring to Mary is not as a Virgin but as the bearer of God, *Bogorodyitsa*.) Jesus is usually portrayed as a mature, bearded judge in regal robes, Mary as a younger but mature mother, often with an almost unsupported, rigidly erect, and swaddled Infant Jesus. There are

2

My usual, and preferred, method of modifying my total ignorance of the national character of the people I am investigating is by long interviews with members of that society. Although clues can be found and hypotheses developed by an analytic reading of books and other symbolic material, I personally prefer to use such material for confirming (or disproving) hypotheses deduced from interviews, and for providing additional evidence.

Who my earlier informants are is usually a matter of chance. I have been fortunate, so far, in always having friends who have had friends or acquaintances of the nationality I am interested in, who have given me introductions. These first informants in turn give me introductions to their compatriots. As the research progresses, I may feel the need for interviewing people who occupy (have occupied) certain positions in their society; in that case I enlist the assistance of anybody whom I think capable of helping me; or, if I know that a person of the type I am interested in exists, write directly. (In the later stages of this current study I combed the North-East United States for wet-nurses—unsuccessfully—for *nyanyas* and for people who had been in a position to make political and commercial appointments.)

many representations of God the Father, again as a bearded man of early middle age, and some strange triune pictures of the Trinity, consisting of three merging and identical faces, occasionally reduced to three noses and four eyes. This choice of sacred images appears congruent with my hypotheses.

Since studies of this nature are inevitably qualitative and not quantitative—to use an analogy from biology, they are anatomic, not taxonomic—and since it is impossible to produce any reliable quantitative and statistical results,[1] I do not pay much attention to the 'sociological' representativeness of my informants, though I try to get them from as many varied social milieus as possible, and of all ages and both sexes. I try to get as much of a 'scatter' as possible, but make no attempt to make this scatter proportionate. In most cases the risk I have to guard against is 'reverse' proportions; often the largest portion of the resident population—the peasants and factory workers—is quite inadequately represented in the migrant population.

I work on the assumption that any individual who has passed his or her childhood and adolescence as a full participant of his culture[2] is a typical representative of his culture and manifests its national character, whatever his or her individual characteristic attitudes, quirks, vicissitudes or occupation may be. This may appear paradoxical, since we are all deeply and intimately aware of the differences between individuals; but in the same way and at the same time, as people acquire their mother-tongue, they acquire their national character. To pursue this analogy further, different people have very different vocabularies and different manners of speaking, some-

[1] Statistics gathered by technicians for other purposes are of course employed when available.

[2] Because of this stress on full participation I refused all informants who were not born members of the Orthodox Church; or, in the case of atheists, whose parents were not born members of this Church.

times different accents; one may use the language fluently and skilfully, while another may barely make himself understood; one may use the language poetically and imaginatively, whereas another may only make flat and dry statements; some may stammer, some lisp, some speak ungrammatically; and each speaker has an individual voice and intonation which his friends usually recognize without ambiguity. It needs a very analytically minded person to be conscious of the fact (so obvious to a foreigner) that he and his friends and family all speak the same language, with its highly complicated and idiosyncratic rules of grammar and syntax, and probably speak it in a way which identifies them by class, or region, or both. Without perhaps full verbalization, people recognize and stress the *differences* of timbre, speech rhythm, and turn of phrase which give each person his speaking individuality; but they completely ignore the far larger *identity* of language and accent which characterizes everyone in the group and the group itself and (linguistically speaking) completely differentiates it from groups of very similar social and individual composition in other societies, and often from similar groups in other regions or classes of its own society.

The fact that a person has learned Russian (for example) as his mother-tongue means that his thoughts and concepts will be limited and defined by the vocabulary and syntax of the language; in certain important ways he will view and interpret the universe differently to the way he would do if he had been brought up with English or Chinese or Esquimaux as his mother-tongue. Further, every Russian is an informant (technically a linguistic informant) on the Russian language; one may have a specialized technical vocabulary, another may speak with a peasant idiom, and so on; but if you want to learn Russian, and know none, any native-born Russian can be your informant or teacher, though you may learn more, and better, and more easily, from some than from others.

Analogies are dangerous traps for the unwary; but I am convinced that in this case the analogy is fundamentally accurate; that every deviation and variety of personal character is a deviation from the norm of the national character; even in the case of the neurotic and the physically handicapped this axiom holds good. Though I know of no work on the subject, I feel convinced that a study of deafness, for example, would show significant differences in different societies in the manner in which this affliction is endured and interpreted, and the way in which the sound of hearing respond to the deaf.

When I have a first interview with an informant, I always give briefly my reasons for troubling them, and on occasion a little of the theoretical background; in many cases I state my sincere belief that the study I am engaged on will tend to promote mutual understanding between their country and ourselves; and I always try to convey, even if I do not state it in so many words, my conviction that each informant has unique and valuable knowledge which only he (or she) is capable of providing. Then, unless the informant has specialized knowledge on which I want to concentrate, I ask some quite general question: usually, in the case of mothers or grandmothers, how they brought up their children; in the case of men, or women without children, details of their schooling. From then on, I let the informant take charge of the conversation, filling in pauses by demands for further clarification; in the main part of the interview I only direct the conversation if the informant is indulging in excessive generalizations or entering political arguments. After a number of interviews, I always have a series of subjects which I want to check with every appropriate informant; if they have not come up spontaneously during the course of the interview, I bring them up at the very end, usually after the interview is formally over, and we have risen from our seats. I count the interview a failure, whatever the information gained, if it has not been for the informants an interesting and stimulating experience, which they wish to repeat in the near future. In most cases the informant's response is rather like Monsieur Jourdain's delighted discovery that he had been talking prose all his life; people are pleased to discover that their 'ordinary' life can be so deeply interesting to a stranger.

Unless I have excessively nervous informants, I take the fullest possible notes (I do not know shorthand); I either have my notebook out at once, or use the first excuse of a foreign word or phrase to bring it out of my pocket. I have acquired the technique of writing—almost illegibly to others, I must confess—without looking down at the paper on which I am writing; none of my attention is distracted from my informant by this note-taking, and, as far as I can tell, it never worries the informant. My preferred situation is to interview two or three or more (up to about six) informants at once; they stimulate and correct one another, forget that I am there, or nearly, and often evoke material which I would not envisage, or of a depth I should be unlikely to reach; and their behaviour towards one another gives valuable additional data. In the case of professional people interviewed alone I like to have a shorthand typist (seated behind the informant and out of sight) to take down the interview *verbatim*. When I have taken down my own notes, I dictate or write as full an account of the interview as possible at the first opportunity.

I take these extremely full notes, always indicating my own questions, and any interruptions, whether from other informants or mechanical causes (telephones, doorbells, &c.), because two of the chief sources for getting hypotheses (as contrasted with data) are metaphors and the free association of ideas;[1] the juxtapositions of ideas or figures of speech have quite different significance if they are spontaneous or if they are elicited. When they are elicited, the means by which they are elicited may also be significant. This concentration on metaphor and association of ideas bears a slight resemblance to psychoanalysis, and would not have been developed without the practice of the psycho-analytic interview; but it is also not unlike the work of the classical detective of fiction, hunting for significant clues among the mass of data presented.

As far as possible, I avoid asking leading questions;

[1] Other topics which I find suggestive are jokes of all kinds, swearing, religious observances, obscenity, preoccupations about health, judgements or criticisms made of other individuals in the same society, criticisms of concrete aspects of foreign cultures.

but an elucidating technique which I have often found useful is the presentation of cross-cultural illustrations, either from the society in which the interview is taking place or from other societies which I know of from reading or investigation, and asking whether the informant's experience contains anything similar.

3

I first became aware of the existence of the practice of swaddling among Great Russians not from an interview, but from a discussion in our group of typical Russian gestures and body movements. In the course of this discussion Margaret Mead interpreted the movements of one of the gesticulating Russians in a way I had failed to and, turning to her, asked, 'X, were you swaddled as a child?' It then developed that all but two of our Russian collaborators (these were children of intellectuals) had been swaddled. It may be of interest to note that, though I failed to interpret the gestures at this meeting, I could, after three months' interviewing, tell at a glance, and with practically no errors, if a Russian had been swaddled as a child: the square set of the shoulders, the 'resting position' of the upper arms against the side of the body, further back than is habitual with people who have not been swaddled, and many symmetrical gestures with the forearms and hands, the upper arms being kept in the resting position—these are the chief indicators of which I am conscious.

I did quite a little interviewing before I got much further information; I found that I had not made my ignorance of Russian character complete enough and had assumed—incorrectly—that mothers would be able to tell me how children were brought up. This delusion was finally shattered one evening when a Russian mother, who was absent from the room watching her little son be put to bed when I arrived, had to go into the child's bedroom a couple of hours later to see if his arms were inside or outside the swaddling. I then discovered that the only people who know articulately about infant care are grandmothers;[1] and the curious fact developed that the birth of a grandchild brought back into conscious memory the treatment the grandmother had given her own children. I also found that though Russians could normally recall very little of their own childhood, if they had a brother or sister some six or more years younger (particularly if of the same sex) they could recall a great deal about the childhood of this younger sibling, and often by deduction of their own.

[1] The social arrangement of linking alternating generations (grandparents and grandchildren) occurs in many parts of the world; it is often symbolized by grandparents and grandchildren using the same term of address to each other. Often the grandparents have the major care of the child after weaning. I do not know of any field-work which has studied societies with such arrangements from a psychological point of view. It would appear that the old and very young are equated by their equal distance from full strength and maturity. Great Russian peasant life would seem to show an echo of such arrangements, with the role of the grandmother, *babushka*, and (to a lesser extent) the grandfather caring for the grandchildren. In the words of the Russian proverb, 'A daughter's children are dearer than one's own'.

Once the fact of swaddling appeared of importance, it was only a matter of application to discover the extent of the practice by extensive interviewing, the analysis of text-books on child-rearing, photographs of children in crèches and the equivalent of questionnaires.[1]

The first thing I noted about the swaddling was the series of rationalizations concerning the injuries that the child would do to itself if it were not swaddled; and from this I developed the hypothesis that 'restraint is un-bearable; yet one has enormous strength and one must be restrained in order to keep from breaking oneself and others'. I had also noted the orgiastic nature of adult Russian gratifications, and made the connexion between this and the fact that babies were unswaddled for nursing. I also noted that, apart from the swaddling, Russian children did not appear to be deprived or disciplined, and connected this with the lack of apparent anxieties in adult Russians of the type to which we were accustomed in Occidental society.

My chief theoretical preoccupation in the first months of interviewing was an attempt to establish a connexion between the attitudes towards political authority and their prototypes in the familial situation. My first inter-views were chiefly with people in the upper castes, and from them I got the account of what I later called the belief in 'patrilineal' and 'matrilineal' characteristics, the fact that the father loved the daughter for her 'mas-culine' characteristics and so on. I pursued this as far as

[1] It should be kept in mind that, except in these late studies on the extent of the practice, information on swaddling was never given in isolation.

it would go, but did not get any results which seemed satisfactory, nor any which explained the social and political phenomena I was documenting. Furthermore, continued interviewing showed the lack of deep affect (judged from an Occidental point of view) of the emotional relations between parents and children, and the fact that the father was a friendly and succouring figure in nearly every case, whereas 'authority' was severe and distantial.[1]

I then developed the hypothesis (which I abandoned with great difficulty) that the prototype of authority in childhood was the *babushka* or *nyanya*, a moody and somewhat sexless figure, distant from the parents in age or caste or both.[2] This might account for the lack of feeling of 'oneness' between those in authority and those under authority and the 'unpredictability' of authority, and I built a number of constructs on this hypothesis. Russians, however, never accepted it willingly; and it left many aspects unaccounted for.

Meanwhile I had collected from interviews, and other sources, a good deal of evidence for what I have called unfocused guilt and hostility; and also the very great use of the eyes for conveying emotion, love, &c. Somebody reminded me of the rather heartless experiments conducted on children by behaviourists during the

[1] I was puzzled for a long time by the figure of the father in *The Brothers Karamazov*. I now think that Father Karamazov is a symbol of 'authority', in its feared and hated aspects, rather than a representation of a 'typical' father. This interpretation of characters as symbols would seem to be valid in a number of cases in Dostoievsky's major novels.

[2] It was at this period that I searched so eagerly for wet-nurses and *nyanyas* to interview.

twenties, when it was found that holding children's legs straight—that is in the swaddling position—made them cry and also made them angry. I then developed the hypothesis that swaddling was painful, as inhibiting spontaneous movements of the limbs[1] and that the infant responded to this pain with rage. I further suggested that this rage was projected and produced guilt or fear; I almost certainly derived this from my contacts with Mrs. Klein, Dr. Rickman, and other psychoanalysts interested in Mrs. Klein's developing ideas some months previously. This hypothesis seemed to account for the diffuse guilt and fear, and suggested that swaddling was psychologically important. I then re-read my interviews to see if I could get any further leads from metaphors or free associations.

On swaddling itself two free associations seemed to me important. Russians refer to swaddling material as 'bandages'; and shortly after talking of children being 'bandaged', more than one informant referred to 'Lazarus lying three days bandaged in the grave'; this connexion of the swaddled baby with a corpse[2] seemed to suggest that there was very strong negative emotion about (being) a swaddled baby. Another woman, trying to explain to me about swaddling, stuck out her legs and crossed her arms on her breast. I asked if the arms were

---

[1] When I first produced this hypothesis I was reminded that one of the alleged tortures imposed by the Russian secret police is to insist on several hours' complete immobility in a rigid position.

[2] In fact, with a resurrectible corpse; but I did not see the full significance of this until after I had developed the hypothesis of infantile depression (see below) and was discussing the evidence with John Rickman.

crossed as she held them. She hesitated and then said, 'No, I think flat, like this [again sticking out her feet and putting her arms flat against her sides]. *You know the Russians put a lot of emphasis on every point*. The young mothers that I knew accepted the propaganda against swaddling but explained why they did the opposite. . . .'

The italicized phrase was one starting-point for the hypothesis of the 'circle of truth' and the importance of the periphery as contrasted with the centre. It made a link with the hypotheses on Truth developed by Dr. Mead and Mr. Calas.

I did not get further clues from the descriptions or discussions of swaddling; but when I re-read my material on authority, particularly on school-teachers and school-children, both interviews and excerpts from Soviet text-books, I was much struck by the wealth of metaphor applied to teachers and their authority which could equally well be applied to swaddling: firm and consistent, weakening softness, neither too tight nor too loose, and so on. The most striking examples out of a great deal of evidence are presented in Chapter IV, section 3. It was from this material that I produced the most novel (theoretically speaking) of the hypotheses: that the prototype of authority was not any figure in the familial environment but the impersonal swaddling. In Chapters III and IV I have presented the conclusions and some of the evidence from my own material; but one of the most telling illustrations was produced by Dr. Leites from his fund of political knowledge; the fact that the chief theoretical quarrel between Lenin and Rosa Luxembourg was on the question whether the workers could develop 'straight' without the tight 'swaddling' authority of the Central Committee.

Once the attention was focused on the importance of swaddling it was possible to make some other deductions directly—e.g. the role of the eyes, the inhibitions on exploring the universe, the role of teething and fantasies of devouring, &c., and others, such as the reason for the apparent enjoyment of unpleasant emotions, more tentatively.

When I had reached this point my work in the United States had to be terminated. I wrote a paper developing the hypotheses in that state, and it was only through a series of accidents that it was not published in that form. In one paragraph in this paper I still clung—rather halfheartedly, it is true—to the figure of *nyanya* or *babushka* as the prototype of authority. I found it difficult to make the intellectual jump of abandoning every human figure in the infantile world; and also I was probably unconsciously loath to consign so much work to my files.

Back in England I did a good deal of further reading and re-reading of Russian literature and history for my own edification; but I did not think of modifying my hypotheses until Margaret Mead came to England for the Mental Health Congress, in August 1948, bringing with her a generous selection of the material which had been collected after my departure by the Russian group in New York. Included in this material were a number of excerpts Dr. Leites had made from classic Russian literature on the exhilaration of rapid movement, the unpleasantness of motionlessness, and the joining of these two emotions in Pushkin's lyric *The Demons*, quoted in

Chapter II, section 2. This material struck me as odd and difficult to interpret; pondering on it, I thought I saw an analogy in the misery of motionlessness to the misery of depressives, and the concepts of Melanie Klein on the infantile 'depressive position'; and I then produced the additional hypothesis of infantile depression as a result of exhaustion from unassuaged rage. This hypothesis seemed to account more adequately for three sets of facts for which we had plenty of data: the pleasure in painful emotions, the fact that Great Russians viewed weakness as absolute and not relative, and 'avalanche fantasies'.

Some weeks later I was invited to participate in an international seminar convened by the Centre Cultural International de Royaumont. Also taking part in this seminar were two young French psychoanalysts of altogether exceptional qualities, Professeur Daniel Lagache of the Sorbonne and Madame Dolto-Marette. I gave them my Russian hypotheses to read, and was enormously encouraged by their response to such unconventional material. Professeur Lagache told me of an analysand he had had who, on account of a childish skin disease, had been swaddled from his fourth to his tenth month, with psychological responses very similar to those I had hypothesized, and which Professeur Lagache had only been able to interpret at the end of the analysis,[1]

[1] This is the only case I have discovered of the psychoanalysis of an adult swaddled in infancy. The only reported case of the psychoanalysis of an Orthodox Russian (the reported presence of Jews as servants makes it uncertain if the patient were a Great Russian) is Freud's 'wolf man'. ('From the History of an Infantile Neurosis' (1918): S. Freud, *Collected Papers* (London, Hogarth

and Madame Dolto-Marette was married to a Russian, who had also been psychoanalysed, and she told me that she thought the construct of the character was correct, though she had explained it on more conventional Freudian lines. Monsieur Dolto subsequently gave me a great deal of most useful confirmatory material.

With this theoretical support, aided by John Rickman's encouragement and collaboration, and egged on by Professor Edward Shils, I decided to suspend the work on which I was then engaged and rewrite the hypotheses in a longer and more detailed form. It was while I was engaged in this task that I produced the latest development (to date) of the swaddling hypotheses: the interpretation of the role of the Leader as a projection of the 'idealized self'. This was developed under the stimulation of Melanie Klein's *Contributions to Psycho-analysis, 1921–1945*[1] which I was reading in the evenings for a review. In her paper on *Mourning and its Relation to Manic-depressive States* (p. 316) she writes:

'In the infant the extreme character both of his sadistic and of his constructive fantasies is in line with the extreme frightfulness of his persecutors—and, at the

Press, 1933), Vol. III, pp. 473 ff.) Apart from the information that the patient was born in a caul, this paper tells nothing about, and makes no deductions from, the experiences of the first year of life. There is too little social information to decide with any certainty which caste the patient belonged to; what does appear untypical in the account given is the (apparently) very small household in which the patient grew up. It may be of interest to note that, in discussing the difficulties of analysing this patient, Freud writes of his 'national character that was foreign to ours' (p. 585). As far as I know, this is the only place where Freud uses the concept of national character.   [1] London, Hogarth Press, 1948.

other end of the scale, the extreme perfection of his "good" objects. Idealization is an essential part of the manic position. . . .'

I do not subscribe to all of Mrs. Klein's views by any means, nor do I wish to suggest that all Great Russians are manic-depressives—it seems to me nearly meaningless to apply psychiatric terms developed to describe deviants in one culture to the norm of another culture —but under the stimulus of this passage I reconsidered my evidence concerning the Great Russians' attitudes towards their Leader, and developed the hypothesis which can be found in the first section of Chapter IV.

4

I was first appraised of the existence of swaddling among the Great Russians by a sudden insight of Margaret Mead's; but had I held more firmly in my mind the concept of the 'culture-area' I should have expected it, instead of being surprised. Swaddling— wrapping the young infant in strips of cloth instead of enveloping it in a loose piece of cloth, clothing it in fitted garments, or letting it be naked—is a very widespread custom; it apparently spreads almost uninterruptedly[1] from the North polar regions to the Mediterranean, the Himalayas, and the Mexican border.

A frequent—and natural—question in response to my

[1] I write this without the complete checking of the data which should ideally be performed.

hypotheses on the influence of swaddling on Great Russian character is to ask why it does not produce similar results on all swaddled peoples. This is a difficult question to answer, for I know of no other comparable researches on societies employing swaddling; all I can do is to point out how, in the instances on which I have some information, Great Russian swaddling is different.

(I) *Amount of body swaddled.* In Central Europe, including France, apparently only the trunk is swaddled; movements of the limbs are not impeded. The Italian *bambino* of classical painting and bas-reliefs has his hands and arms free, and his exploration of the universe is not much impeded.

(II) *Length of time swaddled.* In Central and Western Europe the swaddling is replaced by clothing which allows free movement very much earlier. According to some travellers the swaddling is removed much later—towards the end of the second year—in Albania and Southern Yugoslavia; we know very little about these people; but the stories of blood-feuds, &c., suggest that this swaddling may produce psychological responses of a simila nature to those I have postulated in Great Russians.

(III) *The absence of hunger and other unpleasant internal sensations.* According to one trained informant, Polish peasant babies were as completely swaddled as Russian babies in their first weeks of life, but they also suffer a great deal from hunger, the mothers leaving them behind in the house for many hours while they work in the fields, and, when they do feed the babies, feeding them hurriedly and ungenerously. On theoretical grounds I should expect unpleasant internal sensations to outweigh (psychologically) unpleasant peripheral sensations; it is the Russian baby's physiological contentment which gives such relative psychological importance to the restraints of swaddling.

(iv) *The impersonal handling of the infant and the treating of the infant as strong.* Eastern European Jewish babies are swaddled; but the reason given for this is that they are so weak and fragile that they might otherwise be damaged by clumsy adults, especially the father. This would imply that the child—both swaddled and unswaddled—is handled in quite a different way to the Great Russian infant; and therefore probably has quite different emotional relationships to the adults around him.

(v) *Great Russian babies are unswaddled for nursing.* The contrast between restraint without gratifications and gratifications without restraint is not experienced by those American Indian tribes who employ cradle boards; the infant is only removed from the board for very short periods; all his infantile experiences, pleasurable and painful alike, are connected with restraint.

There are other societies which employ swaddling, about which I know nothing relevant except this one fact; the field of research in national character—or, if every hypothesis is rejected, in the variations in childcare and child-training—is still almost totally unexplored.

APPENDIX II

A NOTE ON THE SWADDLING
HYPOTHESES

BY JOHN RICKMAN

THE SWADDLING hypotheses[1] break new ground in the field of psycho-dynamics. I have no recollection of having read about the influence of swaddling in psychoanalytical or psychiatric literature, nor heard it discussed. In the former there is much reference to frustration of gratification at the breast and in toilet training and so forth, but the effect of the restriction of movement as a specific factor in influencing the development of the personality is, I think, new. Though I am not in a position to criticize this general deduction of a national

[1] Naturally one of the first things I was asked by the originator of the swaddling hypotheses, after he had evolved the idea, was what I had seen of swaddling in Russia. I had to confess that I had not noticed it. The explanations that occur to me are these: first, at that time I had no interest in the treatment of babies, so it was not a detail that would stay in the mind; secondly, the death of babies was so much taken for granted by peasants that they rarely brought them to hospital. (I do not think this was due to my lack of interest.) This supports the author's view that the attitude of the peasants to their children is not the same as in the West. When I did see babies in the hospital or in the peasants' homes they were unwrapped for examination and wrapped up afterwards either in another room or after I had left the house; my ignorance on this point is therefore of no special significance.

character largely influenced by very early experience of individuals I am prepared to accept it pending further evidence. I certainly know of no single factor which affords a better explanation of the Russian character. In addition to the swaddling factor there are others which work in the same direction. The 'diffuse guilt reaction', i.e. guilt not focused upon the relation to one person, may in part be explained by the fact that save for breast feeding the infant is cared for by any one of up to a dozen persons who may be near. Three or four generations usually inhabit the *izba* and anyone from any generation gives a hand, thus the infant grows into a relationship with a community far more than he does in the West. But because of her breast feeding the mother is a central figure as regards gratification. The 'dietetic weaning' is usually ended at about two years, but I have seen children scared at my sudden entry (in that vast mountain of hides) even up to the age of four or five years rush to their mother usually (or to any woman if the mother be not by), and pulling apart the blouse hold the nipple in the mouth, eyeing me the while as I pulled off the layers of fur coats; when satisfied that there was no danger they dropped the nipple and went on with their play.

It is probable that the two factors interact, viz. the swaddling and the fact of being brought up by three generations simultaneously. Since the latter is common to many cultures it is well to give special consideration to the former. Some day we should have a full survey of the influence of swaddling on national character in which record would be made of the following points:

(*a*) the extent of the body restricted, or, in terms of action, the freedom allowed to the various parts of the body. To take but one obvious instance, and that not the most important, the fact that Russian babies can scarcely move any part of their bodies except their eyes helps to answer the question why it is that Russians use their eyes so eloquently. I have not noticed the same use of the eyes in other nationals. I think the swaddling hypotheses have given us an answer.

(*b*) The timing of the swaddling in respect to feeding and its cessation in respect to what I call 'dietetic weaning' would provide another 'scale' by which the 'swaddling cultures' can be arranged.

(*c*) the influence of the swaddling on the parents' relation to the child; I say 'parents' for short, meaning here the people who unswaddle and attend to the child. If the child is turned into a sort of cocoon the impulse to intrude upon it—to see whether it is wet or not, to adjust its pillows, tuck it up, untuck it, and so forth—is obviously in some measure checked. From the point of view of the parents' psychology swaddling prolongs one feature of the intra-uterine state—you can't get at the child or play about with it.

Geoffrey Gorer makes special reference to his debt to Pavlov, Boaz, and Freud. All three authors have influenced his swaddling hypotheses. The alternate constriction and then relaxation with gratification has in it something of reflex conditioning which we associate with Pavlov; the anthropological approach we associate with Boaz, the interweaving of guilt with the texture of the personality (which the other two authors ignore) we

associate with Freud. From that cork-lined physiological laboratory in St. Petersburg which Pavlov ruled
like a Czar an idea which has heretofore been largely
unassimilable in Western psycho-dynamics—though
often uncomprehendingly quoted—is brought into relation with the work of Boaz and Freud.

APPENDIX III

TRUTH AND GUILT

BY JOHN RICKMAN

NOTE: *The late H. W. Massingham, Editor of 'The Nation', with some misgivings published in 1919 two articles of mine, the content of which is incorporated in this Appendix. His misgivings were justified, for it was more than twenty-five years before anyone but myself showed any interest in the ideas expounded in them.*

THE FEATURE of this book which has in my opinion most immediate social importance is the clarification of the *Russian attitude to Truth*. Because there is so little understanding of the profound differences between the Russian and the Western way of looking at Truth there is a tendency for people on both sides of the cultural frontier to ascribe obscurantism and even malice to the other. I have had some experience of the difficulty in getting Western people to see the Russian way of looking at things.[1]

On my return to England from Russia at the end of 1918 I found great confusion of ideas about Russia but very little curiosity about the origins of the striking

[1] I should add that when Geoffrey Gorer wrote this book he had no idea that I had written or spoken on a somewhat similar theme thirty years before.

differences between the Russian outlook and that of the Western Powers. My replies to questions put to me about Russia were listened to with attention, until I suggested that an adequate answer required equal attention to Western ideas for comparison. Then interest lapsed.

It may perhaps be useful to outline briefly how the matter appeared to me at the close of the First World War, since it is unlikely, if the ideas put forward in this appendix are at all correct, that the broad differences which have existed for two millennia will have changed completely in three decades. The view then put forward in many political speeches and in some articles[1] is here expanded (and modified in a few points) because it has relevance to this important problem concerning the difference in attitude towards truth in Russia and in the West.

The argument can be summarized briefly thus:

The Western attitude was greatly influenced by Rome—the Eastern by Athens: Roman lawyers—Greek philosophers: Pauline Christianity—Johannine Christianity: developing individual ownership of the means of production—retention of Communal ownership of the land: Eucharist—Pentecost: Bi- or Multi-party Government—the Mir (Collective opinion) Government.

At the end of the First World War the Central European Powers were attacked from the West and split by 'vertical' (national) divisions, from the East by 'horizontal' (class) divisions: at the end of the Second World War the political rearrangements show signs of following old patterns.

[1] E.g., in *The Nation*, 29 March 1919, and 19 April 1919.

The activities peculiar to man may be viewed as techniques of adjustments made necessary because of his inherent instability. The instability within himself as an individual is mainly the field of study of the psychiatrist, the instability arising through his membership of a community is within the subject-matter of the anthropologist, the sociologist, and the historian. Neither of these disciplines alone can give a full account of the process of adjustment to the instability and, since the adjustments of the individual and the group are interconnected, neither discipline even in its own special field can lay claim to completeness. Out of the full range of possibilities one community, for reasons that are in essentials still obscure, chooses one way of dealing with conflicting tensions, another another; there is probably, if we did but know it, an inevitability in the choice characterizing the community in each case, but this does not imply that one type of community (or national) character can be used for assessing another as being 'right' or 'wrong', 'good' or 'bad'.

With this in mind, and as an exercise rather than as a finished thesis, let us examine the forces other than the purely military that were operating in the First World War to split up the Central European Powers. These forces may be grouped under the names of the two frontiers that were being attacked, Western and Eastern (the latter in this case does not mean Oriental); the two kinds of force have each a long and different history.

Western ways of thought and action have been largely characterized by the inheritance of Rome. In Rome the mental activities of the educated classes employed the mode of thought which characterizes lawyers. The influence of this approach to the problem of human adjustment found its expression in the religious field in the writings of St. Paul[1] where the handling of the problems of spiritual life were thought of in terms of property law, which included in those days the ownership of slaves and their manumission.

In the most sacred rite of the Roman Church, the Eucharist, the thoughts of the devout were directed, when the Divine Essence entered the individual, on the notion of Redemption through the sacrifice on Calvary.

It is unnecessary to stress the general influence of Roman Lawyers on Western culture, but particular attention may be directed to the attack on the Central

[1] Romans i. 14, Paul as a debtor to both Greeks and Barbarians; i. 18, truth held down in unrighteousness; i. 25, the truth changed for a lie; ii. 2, the judgement of God is according to truth; iii. 7, if the truth of God through my lie abounded unto his glory why am I not still judged as a sinner? iv. 4, reward not reckoned as of grace but of debt; ix. 1, I say the truth in Christ, I lie not my conscience bearing witness with me; 1 Corinthians i. 30, redemption through Christ, Galatians ii. 14, when they saw that I walked not according to the truth of the gospel [here a point is argued like a lawyer]; iii. 18, contrasting the inheritance of the law and of promise; v. 3, a debtor to the whole land; Ephesians i. 7, redeemed through blood; i. 11, on being a heritage foreordained; i. 14, on the inheritance through Christ; v. 5, naming what bars a person from inheritance; Colossians i. 12, partakers on inheritance; i. 14, redemption and forgiveness of sins; iii. 24, inheritance as a recompense; Hebrews i. 4, on inheriting a name; ix. 15, Christ as the mediator of a new covenant; 1 Peter i. 4, an inheritance reserved.

Though the Acts of the Apostles was probably not written by Paul but was almost certainly influenced by him it is not inappropriate to refer to Chapter xxvi, verse 18, where there is reference to remission of sins and the inheritance of those sanctified by faith.

The list is by no means complete but it may serve to show how much St. Paul's thought was influenced by Roman Law.

European Powers in the First World War. The lines of cleavage were 'vertical'; state was separated from state with promises of separate treatment in separate treaties of peace. Two thousand years ago the Roman Senate in its political dealings with foreign states used a similar technique.

We can make a generalization by saying that whatever the activity it could always be argued about; basically, intellectual (and spiritual) activity was treated as if it were a step-by-step process of negotiation between contesting clients appearing in the same court. It is not surprising that Western Socialism is commonly thought of as coming gradually.

In contrast to Geoffrey Gorer's point about the Eastern approach to the Truth we might say that in the West the approach is individual, it comes by a slow process of adjustment, that though at moments the grasp of Truth may be felt to be complete, for the most part the notion of 'Living in Truth' is an aspiration rather than an experience, and that we are usually ready to find in other people elements of the Truth which will form the beginning of a negotiation with them. To say this is not to deny the fact that individuals in the West occasionally, but usually only temporarily, experience an 'oceanic feeling' in which their identity with other participants in the Truth is felt to be complete. Above all, the discovery in other people of characteristics which seem alien or even antagonistic to what is regarded as the Truth is accounted for by their imperfect approximation to a viewpoint. The relation to Truth admits of the notion of *quantity* of gradual approximations, whereas the Russians exclude these steps and plump for *quality* —you are in the Truth or else you are outside it, you 'belong' or you don't.

Turning to the Eastern ways of thought and action the comparable point of origin to Rome is Athens. The mental preoccupation of the Greeks was with philosophy and metaphysics, and Christianity derived from this source a different pattern of thought. The relation to God had but little of the personal bargaining which has characterized so much of the spiritual life of the law-ridden West. In Russia the mystics 'belong' in the community to a far greater extent than in the Roman area of influence. The burden of sin is shared by the group of believers and is dissolved by a religious act in which everyone participates simultaneously. Pentecost for the peasants of my acquaintance was the moment in history of supreme significance, not the Last Supper. The Gospel of St. John was their favourite text.[1]

[1] This Gospel shows no sign of Roman influence, at least on my reading of it. To be sure its precision when describing a train of events is lawyer-like, e.g. Chapter ix, where the blind man was made to see, but no use is made of legal ideas. The concepts are almost entirely spiritual or metaphysical: 'The Word was with God and the Word was God', 'The Word was made flesh', 'full of grace and truth', 'the true light which lighteth every man that cometh into the world', 'God is a spirit'. The relation between God and man is expressed in terms of love and identification, belief in the Truth springs from love, and the Truth makes man free from the yoke of sin. The commandment is this: to love one another, 'henceforth I call you not servants . . . but I have called you friends; for all things I have heard of my Father I have made known unto you.'

If one takes the behaviour of the peasants (for instance, that described in 'The Apology' given above) and sets it alongside these quotations from St. John and those given earlier from St. Paul one can see which matches well and which does not.

The conduct of the village *mir* is comparable in the social and economic plane with Pentecost on the spiritual. There is first a discordance of individual opinion in which everyone expresses his personal views, sometimes stridently, sometimes gently; the lack of unanimity to begin with is most striking and there is no sign of party organization. Then with an increasing number of silences (such as occur in groups of chattering people in any part of the world) defined courses of action are mentioned (the speaker claiming no prestige for voicing a policy and none being accorded him) and policy opinions are received with assent or else the hum of talk continues, meaning that opinion is not united. Once opinion is united there is a profound sense of satisfaction and of village solidarity, and the members of the village assembled at the *mir* disperse without a vote having been taken, with no committee formed and yet the feeling that each man knows what is expected of him.

Returning to the end of the First World War: the Eastern attack on the Central European Powers had none of the sharp lawyer-like bargaining characterizing the Western attack but was a diffuse emotional appeal to the masses to join the Brotherhood of Socialist Revolution. Self-abnegation and participation in a mass movement were asked for and in return the peoples of Europe (eventually the world) would receive the strength which comes of human solidarity and eventually communal possession of the means of livelihood. Of course, there were many reasons for the Bolsheviks adopting the world-revolutionary policy; the suggestion here made is that it fitted in with the Russian *mir-sobornost* (Pentecostal) way of thought. It is not surprising that Eastern Socialism is commonly thought of as coming suddenly.

Geoffrey Gorer's theory about the Russian attitude to Truth seems to be supported by the ideas outlined above, but I should like to add that I do not think because of this that the Russians have inevitably a fanatical aggressiveness to foreigners. At present in Russia the people have but little opportunity to measure themselves and their material progress against standards other than their own, for despite the surging oceanic feeling of their political and religious life (I am speaking definitely of the old régime and surmise things have not altered in essentials since) there was a considerable curiosity as to how others lived and thought. I would remind readers of the 'Political Episode' in an earlier section of this book; at the time of the Constituent Assembly there was among the villagers I served a desire to use the political experience of the West as a model. Subsequent events seem to show that the materialistic Kremlin has, like Peter the Great, 'opened a window to the West' but only in respect to physical, not sociological or psychological, techniques. In order to keep their control over the masses the Kremlin rulers have to paint foreigners as beings who are black and themselves as beings who are white.

The greatest difference as I see it between the old régime and the new is in relation to guilt. In the old régime though the Church was so much in the service of the Czar it nevertheless gave the people a different scale of values to that supplied by the Autocracy; Czars could be measured against the myths about the saints.

In the present day the Kremlin (carrying One Party Rule to its logical conclusion) tries to be both State and Church. It decries any pangs of conscience except for breaches of its own rules and denies that its own destructiveness can carry a load of remorse; so far as my experience goes this sounds to me un-Russian and therefore I am not surprised that the political police are busy.

My next point is that the new régime in Russia is far further from an understanding of Western culture than the old. In the old, though there was this mass-action, an all-or-none approach to Truth, the body of Truth, with its acceptance of internal contradictions, included an acknowledgement of the complexity of guilt (one of the points in common between the old régime and the West): the Kremlin, on the other hand, allows of only one kind of sin—disbelief in the complete correctness of its system.

The gulf between the leaders and the led is in certain important respects greater than ever; the internal tension—witness the strength of the political police force—is as great as in the old régime despite a 'people's revolution'. Geoffrey Gorer has outlined a policy for keeping the Russians within bounds, but neither he nor I nor anyone else has put forward a plan to lessen that tension-creating gulf. But perhaps in time the effect of early upbringing, which the Soviet Authorities are trying to westernize, may produce a change in the national character. A peasant, after asking how we did things in the West, said to me when discussing the new régime, 'We peasants will give them thirty years and then see what they make of the job'. We too must exercise such patience before passing judgement upon a way of life that is difficult for us to understand and that conflicts with so much we accept, perhaps uncritically, as right. It is the Russian attitude to Truth that is, of all things, the most baffling. For the Russians, this attitude to Truth is at once a source of strength and an inspiration: for us it usually seems mere confusion. Nothing is harder than to move into the ways of another culture; few things are more important, particularly in a world influenced by a rapid increase in the rate of communications, than a realization of the restrictions which our own culture imposes upon our tolerance of human differences.